E S S E N T I A L

SKIING

A BIBLE FOR BEGINNING SKIERS

ESSENTIAL SKIING

A BIBLE FOR BEGINNING SKIERS

HERB GORDON

Lyons & Burford, Publishers

Printed in the United States of America

Text design and composition by Rohani Design, Edmonds, Washington

Illustrations by Tom Mosser

10 9 8 7 6 5 4 3 2 1

Library of Congresss Cataloging-in-Publication Data

Gordon, Herb.
    Essential Skiing : a bible for beginning skiers / Herb Gordon.
       p. cm.
    Includes bibliograpical references and index.
    ISBN 1-55821-462-3 (pbk.)
    1. Skis and skiing. I. Title.
  GV854.G68 1996
  796.9'3—dc20   96-35069
                                                      CIP

*Dedicated to those
redheaded double-black diamond
demons Hilary and Rebecca
and to Gail, whom
I first met on the
detachable chair lift in the
Poconos Mountains
of Pennsylvania*

Contents

Introduction

When skiing in America was still a death-defying novelty practiced on twisty trails chopped through New England's mountains, and I in my teens, three friends and I drove in my family's square-box Essex across the snow-blown sagebrush plains of southern Idaho from our homes in Pocatello to the towering Sawtooth Mountains. We were eager to learn something about this sport of whizzing down slopes on long slabs of wood. Our objective: Sun Valley, the "eighth" wonder of the world, near a sleepy mining town, Ketchum. Skiing had invaded the West in the glory of this fabled resort.

We had seen newsreel films of the Hollywood stars who cavorted there. We were determined to watch them in the flesh daring the snowy steeps.

Arriving in Ketchum in the early afternoon, we asked an old farmer standing on a corner where the skiers were skiing.

"Oh, them," he snorted. "Them with those fancy duds. Well—you go on up that road"—he pointed toward some low hills—"and that's where them stupid mules do it."

We swung onto the road and drove to a tiny parking lot—in that era skiers arrived by Union Pacific trains—at the foot of Dollar Mountain, with its amazing chairlift carrying skiers up the slopes.

We could only gasp. If we'd only had a couple dollars we could have rented a pair of those polished wooden skis with bear-trap bindings, slipped our hiking boots into them, and . . . skied. No way. No bucks. Not in those days. We watched. We envied.

Climbing back into the car, still dazed, we drove to a nearby cattle ranch to spend the night with one of my traveling companions' cousins. In the morning, after first helping with the outdoor chores—cleaning stables, feeding animals—we gulped a simple Idaho breakfast of steak, eggs, toast, potatoes, oatmeal, pancakes, coffee, and dessert.

We returned to Sun Valley, this time daring to walk carefully through the magnificent lodge, and even to peek into the men's shower room, staring in vain for a glimpse of A Famous Star's naked butt. Then we headed again for Dollar Mountain and gasped once more at the fearless skiers on the snowy steeps. Skiers still ski Dollar, but today it's classified as a learning area.

Driving icy, rutted roads back to Pocatello we agreed that skiing was neat. The future. And we all knew that as soon as we could scrounge a few silver dollars, we'd buy skis and climb the foothills above home to savor the challenge of the sport.

By the following winter, two of us had managed to scrounge the few dollars for a pair of catalog skis with bamboo poles. We had as much knowledge about skiing as anyone we knew—we actually had seen skiers—and bought skis 7 feet long. The prevailing wisdom then was the longer, the better. We couldn't afford bindings. Ours came equipped with toe straps.

Skiing was elemental. You dressed for the weather—woolen long johns, woolen pants, shirt and sweater, a long coat, woolen socks, and hiking boots. Then you sort of cross-country skied to a hill, took off your skis, slung them over your back, and climbed as high as you wanted to ski down. Stopped. Pushed your toes into the leather toe straps, lashed the straps to your ankles with leather thongs so when you fell the skis wouldn't go sailing down the slopes without you, then pointed the skis downhill, and skied.

Straight down!

Carve a turn? Snowplow? Skid to a halt? Nonsense. Who knew any of that stuff? You skied as far as you could navigate upright. Usually, the final stop was smack into a wiry clump of sagebrush.

Someday, I vowed, I'd put some bear-trap bindings on my skis and really go skiing. That "someday" was a long time coming.

I left Pocatello. Time carried me to any number of places and events. An old war. I married, became a father three times over, worked on a couple newspapers, then spent a few years in Washington as a diplomatic correspondent for the old International News Service.

Skiing? Even the desire had faded with the years.

Toward the end of my work in Washington, my son, Gary, roared into the apartment one morning shouting that a friend was moving to California. His dad had a pair of skis he was willing to sell for $10. Couldn't we buy them? Please, Dad. Come on, Dad. Ah, please. Why not, Dad?

So, the Gordons ended up with a pair of skis. Wooden skis with metal edges and bear-trap bindings. They looked interesting sitting in a closet. On a couple reasonably snowy days my son tried them on the front lawn. Not very exciting for him. I didn't even bother.

They were still virtually untouched when my work took me to New York and, eventually, to NBC. The dusty skis cluttered up a small closet in our new suburban apartment. I finally gave them to a local Boy Scout troop. I was no longer an excited teenager. Winters were cold. Skiing was—as it still is—an expensive sport. Why, a day's lift ticket was probably $5. Besides, I was too old to learn.

An editor I worked with was an eager, dedicated skier.

He talked about skiing. He described every weekend ski trip he went on. He invited me to come along—just for one day. Not for me. Why not? Oh, the usual reasons. The same ones most nonskiers use.

Finally, vaguely intrigued by his enthusiasm, but chiefly to shut him up, I agreed to go with him to a small ski area nearby and try it—once again.

We drove up early one morning, following winding roads through the heavily wooded Harriman–Bear Mountain Park, a forest reserve some 90 minutes from New York City, to Silvermine, a "resort" at a mountain at least 300 feet tall. No chairlifts. Skiers could either grab a rope tow or balance their butts against a T-bar to reach the summit.

Warmly bundled, I rented a pair of skis. My courage was enhanced with a gulp of brandy. My feet were wedged into a pair of my friend's old "ski" boots—a double pair of heavy leather lace-up boots, one pair inside the other. Carrying our skis, I followed him across the snow to the rope tow.

"Okay," he grinned. "Stick your feet into the bindings."

I did.

"Now watch. I'll grab the rope and just let it pull me up. Watch." He grabbed. He yelled back. "Come on. Take hold."

How I managed to stay upright all the way to the summit is something I cannot now account for.

I looked down. What a monstrous distance when standing on skis.

My friend edged over. "Follow me," he said. "It's easy."

I tried to ski in his trail. I fell. I bloodied my nose.

He handed me a scrap of tissue to clean it off. "You're doing great," he said.

Somehow I reached the bottom. I looked up at the gigantic peak. I had skied down that entire mountain?

"How do you feel?" he asked.

"Oh, wow!"

I've been skiing ever since.

A couple years later I met my present wife, Gail, on a triple chairlift at Camelback, in Pennsylvania's Pocono Mountains, while on a one-day trip to practice skiing on easy intermediate slopes. This was as far as I'd advanced by acquiring knowledge from friends and "How to Ski" books. Gail was even more of a novice than I . That was the first day she'd ever skied an area with a genuine chairlift.

But this became a winter of serious intent: We took lessons. Mostly in weekend classes at several different ski areas—Mount Snow, Stratton, Bromley.

Our first ski trip to Europe was to fabled Chamonix in the French Alps early the next winter. Staring up at those dramatic heights we quickly agreed on the need to hire a private instructor for three hours a day during the week we were there. Fortunately for our strained pocket-books the dollar was vigorous, the franc weak, and our instructor's cost only a few centimes more than the ski school's. The payoff was gold.

By the end of the week we were cruising behind him down the high intermediate trails, with an occasional stretch of low expert thrown in to keep us in skiing trim.

Two years later our redheaded, identical-twin daughters started "ski-ing" when they were three months old—sleeping in orange crates in a friendly day-care center at Hunter Mountain, in the Catskills—while Mom and Dad tackled the slopes.

As a family, we've skied together ever since: We've tackled the beautiful resorts carved down New England's forested mountains; braved the high slopes of Colorado and Utah and Washington and Idaho and western Canada; and tested our skills on other Alpine slopes in France, Italy, and Austria. Summer vacations? Bah, humbug.

I still can't answer one question: Why did I waste all those winters before rediscovering the challenge, the excitement, and the sheer joy of skiing?

1

Getting Started

This chapter discusses the realities of what's involved in getting started, from setting your own activity level to buying your first pair of skis, and from locating inexpensive housing to ignoring the entire ski industry's idiotic concentration on promoting skiing as a sport only for the young. An how can you convince anyone that you're a skier if you don't know the terminology of skiing? Here's a review of ski terms, from *edging* to *snowplow*, along with descriptions of various lifts, man-made snow, and how to read the ski reports in the newspapers.

ENJOY, ENJOY

A few months after the death of her husband, Joan accepted an invitation from her son to celebrate her 68th birthday at Steamboat Springs in the towering Colorado Rockies where he was a certified ski instructor. Yielding to his urgings, she finally spent one day in a class for beginning seniors.

I first met her two years later when we shared a chairlift to the summit of Old Baldy, the giant Sun Valley ski mountain. She told me that that first lesson had opened a new panorama on life. "I learned I could do something I'd never tried. And it's such a wonderful sport. It fills my winters. I'm always meeting new people."

I recall another first. There'd been a heavy snowstorm earlier in the week and we were off for our first ski trip of the season. It was a special moment for our sparkling, noisy twins: It would be their introduction to skiing. After all, they were 23 months old.

Standing among the eager skiers swirling around the base lodge at Hunter Mountain the girls bounced with joy as plastic skis were tied to their tiny boots. With their mom and I each pulling one, they were hauled up a perilous, snowy slope all of 15 feet long.

At the summit, Mom pointed them downhill. She released them individually. I caught each as she streaked toward the bottom. They giggled with glee over the experience.

"More. More," chanted one. "Me, too," her sister begged. Now dynamic 18-year-olds, they've been ardent skiers since that day.

The golden thread that weaves together the twins and the grandmother is simply this: No one in good health and spirit is ever too young or too old to enjoy the excitement of skiing.

It Is Not Dangerous

To some, the thought of hurtling down perilous mountains on skis, always on the edge of danger, may be the reason for taking up the sport. To others, living on the edge of danger through skiing may be a fascinating concept, but in reality it's the very reason they don't head for the slopes.

Even a casual discussion with your nonskiing friends or mine about why they don't take up the sport evokes protests that it's too dangerous. Ask them. You know what they'll say: "Oh, no. I could get hurt." "I'm too old." "Hey, I'm not about to ski off a damn cliff at my age and break a leg." "Oh, God, I wonder if I could even get up, falling down all the time."

After more than 25 years of skiing I've known personally only a few skiers who suffered injuries from falls. One was me! Mine occurred when I stumbled over a rope while edging backward toward a chairlift and seriously sprained my wrist.

Then there are those who turn away from skiing because of the erroneous assumption "real" skiers must always be 20-year-olds in superb physical condition—or they couldn't go racing down the mountains like that, could they? We've all heard such expressions as: "Ah, come on. I'm not built like an Olympic athlete." "I've seen the pictures." "Yeah. Skiing down those long mountains, up to their noses in snow. You've gotta be in great shape to do that."

These comments underline the turnoff that an incessant parade of out-of-this-world dramatic stories and sensational pictures by the entire ski industry in magazine articles, ads, brochures, and television features arouses in most nonskiers—or even mature once-upon-a-long-time-ago skiers—and may help explain why the growth of skiing has been flat for the past half-dozen years.

In truth, 90 percent of the over-25 skiers on any mountain or at any resort at any time don't remotely approach the dynamic level of such skiing or possess the physical strength to do it.

The ski resorts themselves are also excessively concerned with catering to young skiers—especially the under-18 crowd—on the theory that "these are the skiers of tomorrow." Of course they are. Most adult skiers today started when they were in their teens. But the eager young teenagers who go skiing today are on the slopes because Mom and Dad take them. The resorts only imperil the sport's growth by their undue infatuation with tomorrow. The need today is to focus on what adults—who pay the bills—want and enjoy and can afford, from the slopes to the cafeterias.

Enjoying Winter

A reason adults often cite for why they're not involved with the challenge, thrills, and pleasure of skiing is that they "hate the cold."

I, too, hate being cold. But I know, as every skier from granddaughter to grandma knows, that if you eat and dress appropriately for the cold—and this may come as a surprise—you really can be comfortable on a winter day. I have some down-to-earth advice later in this book about how genuinely simple it is to avoid the frigid chills when the temperature plunges and you're enjoying yourself on the snowy slopes.

Now, however, I'd add an argument to sway the winter-haters into sampling skiing: It is a cold-weather sport. Winter is an absolute fact of the seasons. But participate in an activity you can enjoy in the winter and, suddenly, it's a season you look forward to. Ice fishing. Sleigh riding with the kids in the park. Winter photography. Ice boating. Snowshoeing. Making snowmen. Skiing.

Ah, there are some wonderful pleasures that only are found in winter's snow.

Set Your Level

Skiing is a challenging sport. The vital reality, however, is that it's a sport in which you set your own level of challenge. You're not part of a team battling another team. You don't compete with anyone else. Skiing is a sport with only one winner—you. And you win by skiing

- on your own terms,

- at your own pace,

- at the level you choose.

If you appreciate the long, gentle green runs, that's where you ski. If the steeper blues are the trails for you, ski them. Go to the top of the perilous mountains. Stay on the low slopes. Hurtle down the steeps, or cruise easily. You make you own choice.

If you become a gung-ho enthusiast, the kind of skier who can't wait to grab the first lift up in the morning and reluctantly hangs up your skis only when the lifts close, it's your preference. Or you can make it a relaxed sport. Stroll into the base lodge at midmorning to enjoy a cup of coffee and a croissant before you even consider heading out to that high-speed, detachable quad chair. Take only a couple runs before it's time for a long lunch and sitting in the sun on the lodge deck to enhance your tan.

The activity level you put into skiing is like that you put into a trip to the beach. You decide how often, and for how long, you want to splash in the waves, or lie indolently in a beach chair.

You do it your way.

Costs

Nonskiers often attribute their lack of interest in skiing to the cost.

There's no ignoring the fact that, like any sport—have you played a round of golf lately? bought a new fishing pole? rented a mountain bike for a weekend of mountain climbing? or even leased a cabin on the shore of a lake for a relaxing week doing nothing?—alpine skiing can chew up dollar bills faster than our dog, Brandy, chews up a bone. But only if you fling prudence into the winter sky. It's also possible to keep the expense of skiing to a respectable minimum. This applies to every aspect of the sport, from equipment to places to stay and play.

Getting started is more exciting than expensive. Costs involve three items: admission tickets, equipment, and housing.

Tickets are highest priced on weekends. For short trips, tickets are cheaper midweek. The per-day cost drops substantially for a one-week ski junket.

As far as ski-school costs go, the single weekend lesson is the most expensive. Costs drop during the week, and a five-day learn-to-ski ticket package is the lowest priced of all.

As far as rental equipment goes, the same weekend, midweek, or week-long rental rules apply here, too.

The never-ever skier has two choices: buy or rent. Until you're convinced skiing is going to be a part of your life, rent your skis (they come equipped with bindings), boots, and poles. All resorts have rental shops. Although their charges may be higher than those of off-the-mountain rental shops, if something goes wrong with the rental equipment you can rectify it quickly at the mountain.

A single day's rental will be about one-third higher if you select new equipment from a demonstration rack rather than the standard rental skis.

Housing

To some of us, a ski-in, ski-out condo at the base of the mountain, with a heated outdoor swimming pool and a private jacuzzi, is what skiing is all about. Others may choose an elegant hotel, a cheerful singles-only chalet, or an inexpensive house with four bedrooms that can sleep as many as are able to crowd into the beds and on the floor.

Virtually every ski resort has its own housing bureau whose staff will attempt to find precisely the facilities you're looking for. However, if they can't fulfill your needs, whether for quality or price, another excellent way to locate housing in the resort area of your choice is to make a telephone call to the nearest chamber of commerce. The local folks know where the housing bargains really are.

Remember, the price of housing is usually inversely proportional to its distance from the base lodge, so you may have to find your own transportation from that great, inexpensive home you rented for the 15-mile trip to the nearest lift.

Both ski tour operators and ski areas offer total packages, including lessons, rentals, bedrooms, and meals, priced well below what you'd pay for each item separately. However, do your homework. You may turn up even better bargains if you have the time to do the digging.

TALKING SKI TALK

For those intrigued by the excitement of learning how to ski, it's also necessary to know the basic terminology of the sport. After all, it might be a little disconcerting for an awkward novice to be told to "follow the fall line" when falling is precisely what she's attempting not to do.

The fall line, obviously, is not for falling. It's simply the steepest way down a slope; it's the route a ball would take rolling down the run. This is the route the ski instructor wants you to ski when he calls out: "Ski the fall line."

General Ski Techniques

Here's a glossary of a few tidbits of ski language really designed to:

- Help you move from reading about skiing to actually skiing, and/or

- Convince those around you (when you happen to drop the terms lightly into a conversation) that you're part of that elite crowd that dares only the great ski slopes.

Edging. The maneuver in which the weight of the skier is on the edge of the skis. The weight can be placed so that the same edge of each ski is dug into the snow, or so that both inner edges are dug into the snow.

Traversing. Skiing across the fall line, not down it. The traverse almost always involves edging, pressing the uphill edge of each ski into the snow.

Slalom or Linked Turns. Skiing downhill in a series of curves. The tracks left by slalom skiers on a field of virgin powder make attractive pictures in ski magazines.

Schuss or Schussing. Pointing the skis down the fall line and whooshing straight down is a maneuver used deliberately by experts and inadvertently by novices. The experts make it safely to the bottom.

Snowplow. Spreading the skis so the tips are almost touching and the tails are spread wide apart. Used by novices in stopping.

Snowplow Turn. Shifting the weight to one ski in a moving snowplow position and going into an easy turn.

Stem or Stem Christie. Halfway between a snowplow turn and the parallel.

Parallel. This is what novices will be doing when they finally learn to carve turns with skis parallel throughout the curve.

Telemark. A turn used by downhill skiers or cross-country skis. The skier adopts a sort of kneeling stance with his outside ski leading, his inside trailing. In the old days, this was how all skiers turned. Then they invented stiff boots, step-in bindings, and skis with steel edges.

Extreme. What gutsy skiers, who are bored with skiing down the steepest trails at the resort, do: They liven things up by leaping off cliffs, hoping to land on a patch of snow larger than their skis.

Trails
Levels of Difficulty
Ski areas throughout the world post color codes on the runs to indicate their degree of difficulty. The basic American system is:

Green Circle—easy or beginner terrain.

Blue Square—moderately steep slopes for intermediate skiers.

Black Diamond—steep runs for advanced intermediates and experts.

Two Black Diamonds—the steepest. Trail signs often include such words as FOR EXPERTS ONLY. Believe!

Yellow Triangle—areas to be avoided for a variety of reasons, such as the presence of major bare spots, ice, or other unsafe conditions.

In Europe, trails are marked green for easy terrain; red for moderate to low expert levels; and black for expert. A red triangle with a black border means that a trail ranges from top expert to extreme.

Neither mountain slopes nor the ski runs on them have the same degree of decline from top to bottom. Thus, a green run may have short sections that are really intermediate. And the intermediate may have some drops that could be classified as expert. At the same time, be aware that an expert run may start out almost as an easy green; around the bend or over the hill, though, the steeper pitches begin.

Types of Trails
Ski Trails also are known as *slopes*, or *runs*, in the United States.

Pistes are what you ski in Europe. Our advanced skiers may head "off trail" to ski areas not maintained. In Europe, they go "off piste."

Bowls are generally treeless slopes without specifically groomed runs.

Glades are a more challenging way to ski to the bottom of a mountain: You ski through the trees rather than down the open runs. Glade skiing is only for skiers who can whip their skis around one hairpin turn after another. Some resorts clear out the underbrush; others leave the skiers to find their own brand of fun challenging the underbrush and trees.

Moguls or Bumps. These are the mounds of snow that cover well-used slopes. The terms are used interchangeably. As skiers curve their way down the slopes, on each turn their skis kick up a slight mound of snow. After a few hours of this the little mounds become big mounds, known as moguls. As the moguls get bigger, the skiing gets tougher.

Grooming. To most skiers this is the most important thing a ski area can do to turn every trail into a slope of joy. It means smoothing out the trails—carved into bumps and moguls by skiers or after a heavy snowstorm—with snowcats, caterpillars that drag an unusually wide metal slab behind them. Special snowcat equipment is used to grind up icy snow and convert the crud into a skiable surface.

Although some grooming may be done during the day, grooming machines usually roar up and down the slopes after the lifts shut down. All night long you can stare up at the snowy heights and see the headlights of the 'cats as they roam the mountain. For those who love the thrill of fast, smooth trails, get on them early.

While grooming is almost universal on green and blue trails, most resorts also groom some of the blacks. An increasingly popular technique is to groom only one side of a black run—leaving the mogul side for the experts and the smooth slope for the skilled intermediates who can handle the pitch but not the bumps.

Though once frowned upon among the grim "ski-it-like-it-is" Europeans, grooming is now becoming as widely and expertly practiced at most Alpine resorts as on the slopes of New England or the Rockies.

Trail Maps. These show all the regular runs at a resort. The trails are usually depicted in color to indicate whether they're easy, intermediate, or rough and tough. Maps come in two sizes: the small kind that slips into your jacket pocket; and—usually at the base area but often at the top of the mountain as well—the huge billboard kind. Larger ski resorts indicate on the billboard current conditions—that is, which trails are open or closed and which ones were groomed overnight.

Vertical. Descriptive information about every ski area always includes three elements—the base elevation, the summit elevation, and the vertical, or difference between the two. The vertical has nothing whatsoever to do with how steep the runs are. But a higher vertical generally means longer and more runs of all types, from green to double black.

A huge trail map at Park West, Utah. Lights indicate whether trails are open, groomed, or closed.

Most North American resorts have a vertical somewhere between 1,500 and 2,500 feet. A dozen exceed 3,000 feet. The verticals of Europe's Alpine ski areas generally range from 4,000 to 6,000 feet.

Lifts

Ski lifts are the answer to generations of skiers' prayers for an easier way to get to the top of a mountain to enjoy a wild run down than trudging up on foot, carrying skis, or sweating blood skiing uphill with skins attached to the bottoms of the skis so they wouldn't slip backward.

Lifts come in various styles:

Rope Tow: A primitive form of lift, the rope tow is occasionally found at beginner areas. It's an endless rope looped around a power source at one end and a revolving wheel at the other. Skiers edge up alongside, tuck their ski poles under one arm, and grab hold of the moving rope, which pulls them uphill. The first lifts up narrow, icy New England trails were rope tows, with the jacked-up back wheel of a Model T Ford truck providing power.

Poma Lift: This is a pole, dangling from an overhead cable, with a rounded seat at the bottom. Skiers tuck the seat between their legs and let it pull them uphill. They don't sit on the seat.

T-Bars: It looks like an inverted T hanging from an overhead cable. The T-bar is designed for either one person or two at once. The T crosses the skiers' butts and pulls them uphill. They don't sit on the bar.

Chairlifts: Chairlifts were invented in 1936 by an engineer employed in building Sun Valley. Several years earlier he'd built banana lifts to carry stalks of bananas, hooked onto an endless cable, from the docks to the deck of a freighter. He thought that a similar system, using chairs instead of hooks, could carry skiers to the top of a mountain. When Sun Valley opened, so did the first chairlift in the world.

Waiting to board a detachable quad chairlift.

Herb Gordon

The original lift had single chairs facing sideways. Chairlifts now generally carry from two to four skiers.

Detachable Chairlifts: The latest improvement in lifts is chairs that detach from the fast-moving overhead cable and slow to a crawl as they move through the loading area. This makes it easy for a skier to get on. As the chairs leave the loading area they snap onto the cable. The seats detach at the summit, moving slowly through the unloading area, making it simple for the most novice of skiers to stand up and slide off. The empty chairs then rejoin the main cable for a swift trip back to the impatient skiers at the base of the mountain.

In addition to being simple to get on and off, detachable lifts have another advantage: They travel at a far greater speed than do standard lifts, substantially shortening the ride to the summit.

Four-passenger detachable quads are the most popular of these lifts, but some seat only three, and a few seat six.

Cable Cars. These are enclosed cars that, using the same principle as the detachable chairlifts, usually carry from four to eight skiers. At Killington, the cable cars are not only individually painted in attractive patterns but also heated and enlivened with music.

Gondolas. More popular in Europe than the United States, these large cable cars haul anywhere from a couple dozen to a hundred or more passengers at a time. There are two gondolas on an endless cable. The cars come to a full halt simultaneously, one at the base and the other at the sum-

Herb Gordon

Cable car at a resort in Chamonix. A high-altitude cable car that services only black diamond trails.

Herb Gordon

Gondola at Whistler Mountain, Whistler/Blackcomb, British Columbia.

mit, to load or discharge skiers. Eager skiers know they're halfway to the top when the two cars rumble past each other.

In addition to all its other lifts, Tignes, in the French Alps, also hauls skiers on an underground train, similar to the New York subway, to one major summit. The train never has to stop simply because of high winds or heavy snows.

Evacuation. When some grinning gremlin stops a lift with a mechanical or electrical breakdown, this is how the stalled passengers are removed. The gremlins work best, naturally, on cold days with high winds when every chair is filled with skiers. Such accidents are a rarity. But if, on the remote chance, it happens to you, not to worry. Sit still. Be patient. From one end of the resort to the other trained personnel, ski patrol members, and ski area staff are swiftly mobilizing to get you off safely.

On chairlifts evacuation is only a matter of slinging a rope over the cable, with a gaming chair on one end. The chair is hauled up to the level of the skiers. Each skier, in turn, slips onto the chair and is carefully lowered to the snow, given a broad pat on the back, something hot to drink, a free one-day pass, and then helped down the mountain. Only once in 20 years was I evacuated. The three-person chairlift jammed. It took the rescue teams two hours to reach our chair, while we swayed over a 60-foot chasm. We were the last ones evacuated. The three of us who'd gotten aboard as strangers became intimate, if chilled, friends, as we alternately joked, cried, shivered, prayed, and waved at our struggling rescuers while they emptied the chairs both in front of and behind us.

No skier on any type of lift at any ski area anywhere in the world of skiing has ever been left to sway forever in the windy skies when the lift suffered from paralysis. On rare occasions passionate skiers who grabbed a moving chair for one more run after a lift officially closed for the day have found themselves swaying all night on a lift that wouldn't start moving until dawn.

Ski Patrol

National Ski Patrol

These are the skiers in the distinctive outfits with the large red cross on the back who cruise the mountains to lend a helping hand when trouble arises. They're trained in emergency lifesaving and perilous rescue techniques.

Courtesy Patrol

Many ski areas have courtesy patrols whose members also cruise the mountains to answer questions, reunite lost kids with lost parents, and stop reckless idiots on skis. Some ski areas employ their courtesy patrollers; others offer free skiing to trained patrol members who help out on busy days.

Man-Made Snow

When a ski area with an average winter snowfall of 300 inches has a year whose total snowfall is 30 inches, it can still keep its slopes open for skiing through that miracle of winter, man-made snow. With the discovery that a fine mist sprayed under pressure into air at or below the freezing mark would turn into snowy crystals, dependable skiing from Thanksgiving to mid-April became a reality.

Until a few years ago there was a tendency among western resorts to belittle the snowy eastern playgrounds because "they have to make snow." Snorting ceased when shifting weather patterns made it clear that, even in midwinter, Colorado and California and Idaho and Utah resorts without the capacity for snowmaking could only moan when muddy bare spots

Skiers ride above a man-made snowstorm at Hunter Mountain, New York.

Herb Gordon

began to show through their thinly covered slopes in January. Bring on the snow guns.

The roaring snow guns originally planted along the sides of the runs produced a heavy snow easily distinguishable from natural stuff. These have long since been replaced by new-style guns and high snow towers, and today's man-made snow is amazingly light and powdery—though still never as fluffy as the new-fallen natural stuff.

Reading Snow Reports

Snow conditions are widely published in newspapers, and broadcast on both radio and television stations, and reported on the Internet. Are the reports believable? Absolutely! However, be aware that conditions may change abruptly because of swiftly shifting weather patterns or exceptionally heavy trail use.

(Of course, every skier has arrived at a resort with bare spots showing only to hear others saying: "Oh, man. You should have skied here last week. Wow. But great." Or has left a ski area with half the trails closed due to lack of snow only to turn on the car radio on the drive down the access road and hear: "Heavy snows beginning this evening.")

Here are the snow condition terms and definitions used to indicate what ski conditions are like:

NS—New Snow. The average accumulation of natural snowfall in the past 24 hours, or continuously for more than a day, from the summit to the base.

ABD—Average Base Depth. The average depth of snow over an entire ski area.

PSC—Primary Surface Condition. The snow conditions that exist over at least 70 percent of an area.

SSC—Secondary Surface Condition. The next-most-prevalent conditions, over at least 20 percent of the terrain.

PDR—Powder. Cold, new, loose, fluffy dry snow.

PP—Packed Powder. Powder snow, either natural or machine made, that has been packed by grooming machines or traffic. It's no longer fluffy, but it's not hard.

HP—Hard Packed. Snow that's been very firmly packed by grooming and wind. You can plant a pole in it, but this takes more effort than with packed powder.

MGS—Machine-Groomed Snow. Loose, granular snow repeatedly groomed by power tillers. Its texture is halfway between LSGR and PP. Some of it has been so pulverized that its texture is like powdered sugar.

WETSN—Wet Snow. Powder or packed-powder snow that has become moist due to a thaw or rain; or, snow that was damp when it fell.

WETPS—Wet Packed Snow. Natural or machine-made snow that was previously packed and then became wet, usually from rain.

LSGR—Loose Granular. Powder or packed powder that's thawed then refrozen and recrystallized; or been sleeted on. LSGR can also result from the machine grooming of frozen or icy snow.

FRGR—Frozen Granular. Often misunderstood, this terms refers to a hard surface of old snow formed when granules freeze after rain or warm temperatures. You can stick a ski pole in its surface.

WETGR—Wet Granular. Loose or frozen granular snow that becomes wet after rain or high temperatures.

ICE—Icy. An icy, hard, glazed surface caused by freezing rain, ground-water seeping into the snow, or the rapid freezing of saturated snow. The surface ice will chip. It won't support a ski pole.

VC—Variable Conditions. This term is used when no primary surface condition can be determined. Trails may encompass a range of conditions—parts may be PP and LSGR, for example.

CORN—Corn Snow. Common in the spring. Granules that are large and loose during the day freeze together at night, then loosen up again on a warm day.

WBLN—Wind-Blown powder or granular snow that forms a packed base.

SM—Snowmaking. The guns are roaring to cover the bare patches from the last thaw.

NS—Night Skiing. A romantic way to enjoy powder trails by moon-light—aided, of course, by field lights.

KM—Kilometers. Alpine runs are measured in miles; cross-country ski trails are measured in kilometers.

XC—Cross Country. This term indicates that a ski resort also has groomed, or marked and maintained cross-country trails.

CRUD—A word that never appears in snow reports. It's plain lousy snow. Icy or muddy. Chunks of frozen granular and bare spots. Rocks and roots sticking up above the thin cover. Borrow an old pair of skis to ski crud.

SC—Spring Conditions. Usually corn snow. Icy in the morning, mushy in the afternoon. You take your chances in the spring, but then it's also coming March and flowers, and in New England farmers have drawn the sap from the maple trees and are boiling it down over wood fires to make the most delicious syrup ever poured on steaming pancakes dripping with butter.

Spring days are why the gods gave us spring skiing.

Crazy things happen on the trails. Skiers doff their down-filled costumes. Some opt for shorts and T-shirts, and some go further.

It was a warm Easter Sunday at Killington. We were standing at the base of a lift and heard a curious clamor of voices far up the slope. The voices grew louder. And then we could see him, hurtling down the mountain, leaping from mogul to mogul, carving turns with the smooth skill of an expert.

Naked as a jaybird without feathers. Wearing only boots and gloves and ski goggles.

The roar followed this demidemon of snow down the mountain. In a final burst of speed he rocketed into a group of friends, a blanket spread wide to catch him and cloak his 15 minutes of glory.

Yes, crazy, wonderful things happen in the spring.

WHEN IT'S BUYING TIME
Clothing

You may feel more glamorous with a neat ski outfit on, but you really don't have to spend the money on one to get started. For that first trip, just dress as warmly as you would on any cold winter day. You'll obviously need a short down or man-made fiber filled jacket, and honest ski pants. If you can't find a pair hanging in a closet, borrow or buy.

When you decide to buy remember that styles of ski outfits for both sexes change faster than the seasons. This, of course, makes it an expensive sport for those who like to stay on the cutting edge of chic. But it's also a great asset for those willing to buy last year's fashions at substantial savings.

Style, however, is not what keeps you warm on a winter day. That's due to the quality of the material used and the manner in which the garment was made.

When the urge to slip into your own ski gear becomes irresistible, and it may well do so even before your second day on the slopes, know what you're actually getting for the amount you rack up on your credit card.

I've whipped up a heavy snowstorm of information about both men's and women's ski clothing, from long johns to the stuffing in a jacket, in Chapter 4, on keeping warm in cold weather. Read it before you buy.

Après wear is another matter. There's only one fiat: Casual.

EQUIPMENT
Boots

Once you're bitten by the urge to own, the first item on your list should be boots. No rental pair is ever as comfortable. At the same time, a boot that fits properly for your skiing ability—whether a rear-entry model or the kind with front buckles—will give you better control over your skis no matter what your level of experience.

For novices who can ride a chairlift, link wedge turns, and stop when desired, a soft-flexing boot is generally recommended for the first ski season. This boot will not only forgive your mistakes but also enable you to ski better and learn faster. However, I doubt you'll remain with this soft boot after your first season. Boots in this category are the least expensive.

Next come the boots for advanced novice/low intermediate skiers who can handle the green trails comfortably but have some difficulty controlling speed on the steeper blues. These boots have a soft flex but are more sophisticated than the beginner-level boot. They're designed for comfort and work well at moderate speeds on groomed terrain. This is really the first boot I'd recommend.

By the time you can ski a blue run with moguls and handle groomed blacks at moderate speed, you've moved into the most popular boot models, the so-called sport boots. These have a moderate flex and are warm and comfortable.

Boots for the really good recreational skier who exults in skiing a wide range of slopes are similar to those for experts, but they usually have a wider last and a softer inner boot, with fewer microadjustments than are available for the mountain experts.

When the only thing stopping you on the mountain is lack of snow, you've hit the expert level. The boots for this category of skier have a variety of microadjustments, stiffer plastic shells, and a firm inner lining to provide a lightening-quick response. These are almost all front-entry boots with four or five buckle adjustments.

Listen to the experts when shopping for boots. Check the specifications and recommendations given in the annual buyer's-guide issues of the ski magazines and know which boots you're interested in *before* you walk into the ski shop. Next, tell the salesclerk how well you ski now and whether you're aggressively pushing to improve your skill level, or are quite satisfied with your present one.

Even if the ski shop carefully measures your foot, there's no gadget that can predict the perfect fit for you. Always try on at least two or three different makes of boot in your category. Another aid to judging a boot is wearing two different boots, one on each foot, while walking around inside the shop. After selecting your boots arrange with the shop to let you wear them around the house for a few days to make certain they're a good fit and, if not, to take them back and return your money.

It's more difficult for a woman to get a proper fit in a ski boot than a man simply because not all manufacturers actually design boots for women; some simply mark smaller men's boots as women's models. For more about women's boots read the section of Chapter 5 on women skiers.

When you rent a pair of ski boots from a well equipped shop, such as this one at Hunter Mountain, they will actually have your right size, and in both male and female models.

Herb Gordon

SKIS

Ski design constantly undergoes changes in the endless effort of manufacturers to produce a better ski for every skier's objective on the slopes. Skis are specifically designed for a variety of users. There are skis for racers, extreme skiers, recreational skiers, novices, and powder hounds.

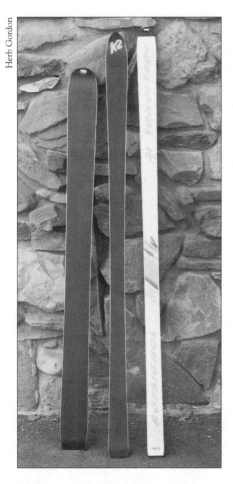

Herb Gordon

The newest designs in skis are the highly touted parabolic or "hourglass" skis, sometimes called "Q-tips." These have received rave reviews from experts and ski magazines—and from this skier. Resorts are stocking them for rentals, though at a premium.

Parabolics make skiing easier for everyone, from novices to top experts. Novices can learn parallel turning more quickly, intermediates who have trouble turning quickly can begin to use their edges to carve turns, and experts can have fun with less physical effort. While some find that the skis have less holding power on steep and icy runs, and that the fat tips are a bit cumbersome on moguls, they have a super reputation for cruising on both soft and groomed runs and blasting through crud.

The new parabolic ski, center, with a wide tip, narrow at the waist, and a wide base is promising to replace both a standard configuration, on the right, and a wide ski especially designed for skiing deep powder snow.

Mike Porter, director of Vail-Beaver Creek ski schools, said: "The development of the parabolics is comparable to the plastic boots that replaced the double-leather boots, and the metal skis that succeed the original all-wood skis." Paul Brown, director of skiing at Sugarbush, said: "Once skiers get used to the fat tips and learn to put the skis on edge, the lights go on!"

The secret of the hourglass ski is that the side cut, or spot where the ski narrows between tail and tip, is narrower than in the standard ski, while both the tip and tail are much fatter. Because the middles of the skis are narrower, they're more flexible. This means the skier's own weight is enough to bend the ski to put its entire edge in contact with the snow. This virtually self-creates a carved turn. Regular skis demand more pressure and effort to make a clean arc in the snow.

My own experience with parabolics took place on a particularly beautiful, warm spring day. Warm enough, in fact, that some skiers were wearing shorts. Not a heavy jacket was to be seen. The snow conditions were less than ideal—sort of softish in the morning, then slushy by midday.

The length of skis is measured in millimeters, not inches or feet. I normally ski 190s, or about 6'4". Irwin Mallory, director of Emilio's Ski Shop at Hunter Mountain, who provided me with demo parabolics, recommended 180s.

It took me a couple hours to learn how to handle skis that turned quickly and easily on snow that would have been difficult to maneuver on with my regular skis. The wide shovel, or tip, of the parabolics slid unusually well through the slush.

By the end of a day's trial, the parabolics had won me over, and my choice for my next pair of skis.

However, whether you pick a traditional design or an hourglass model, choose the ski that's best suited to your style and skill level on the mountains.

My firm recommendation is to not only review the annual buyers' guides but also actually try the ski or skis of your choice on the runs. In other words, don't put out the bucks for new skis simply because a ski salesperson "knows what's best for you." A wide variety of demo skis can be rented from well-equipped ski shops at most resorts. You may find some satisfaction in knowing that they shop will probably deduct the demo charge if you end up buying a pair there.

Regardless of whether you're a dramatic, extreme skier or you simply enjoy the pleasure of the sport, the type of skiing you intend to engage in and the length of your ski are both significant factors in your choice.

To help skiers make a wise choice, *Ski* magazine has created a chart it calls TAKING YOUR MEASURE to answer the endless puzzle of which length of ski is right for you. Add up your points and your score will equal or come very close to the length that experts recommend for you in traditional skis.

If you scored over 200 cm for man, or 190 for a woman, look for a racer or all-mountain ski. If you scored 185–200 cm for a man, or 175–190 for a woman, look for an all-mountain, mogul, or all-mountain value ski. If you scored under 185 cm for a man, or 175 for a woman, choose a value ski (that is, a ski for a moderate intermediate). However, if you choose a

Your Skill Level

(See description on page 68–70)

9–10	50 points
8	48 points
7	45 points
5–6	43 points
3–4	40 points
1–2	35 points

Your Weight

Over 200 lbs.	52 points
181–200	50 points
161–180	49 points
141–160	48 points
121–140	45 points
101–120	43 points
81–100	40 points
61–80	35 points
60 or less	30 points

What type of terrain do you usually ski?

Long, cruising trails	50 points
All terrains	48 points
Deep snow and crud	47 points
Moguls	47 points
Easiest runs	40 points

How do you ski?

Mostly fast, long turns	57 points
All types of turns	53 points
Mostly quick, short turns	50 points
All turns conservatively	42 points
Shakily	35 points

TOTAL POINTS _____ This is your recommended ski length in centimeters (cm).

parabolic ski the experts recommend one slightly shorter—from 7 to 10 cm shorter—than a traditional ski.

Bindings

Modern skiing actually began with the development of bindings that locked a boot onto a ski. The binding had two important functions. First, it enabled skiers to control the way a ski moved, thus permitting them to develop edging and turning. Second, it released the boot from the ski in a hard fall—a rather important function, because if the binding didn't release when the ski turned left and the leg turned right, the snapping sound was gruesome.

Even the earliest bindings did release the leg in most falls, but the ski's sudden freedom meant chasing a loose ski down the mountain. To keep the ski reasonably close at hand in a fall, until only a few years ago it was customary to tie the binding to the boot with a leather thong. There was only one disadvantage to this method: The flailing ski held by the thong could easily smack some tumbling skier with stunning force.

Then the modern brakes were invented. Quite simply, these are two spring-mounted prongs held against the ski when the boot is locked into the binding. In a fall, if the skier pops out of the binding, the prongs spring out and dig into the snow, keeping the ski reasonably close to the skier but without the danger of a loose ski held by thongs whopping you on the head. The modern binding-and-brake combination has all but eliminated the no-longer-justified fear of breaking bones in a snowy tumble.

The modern ski "brake" is a pair of prongs which, when the ski comes off, digs into the snow and stops the ski from flying off into outerspace.

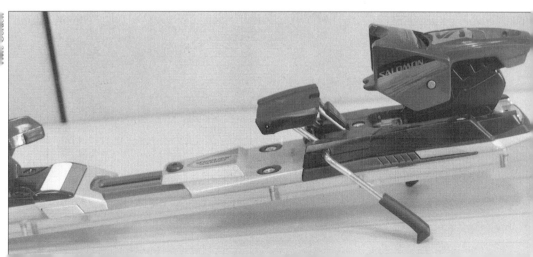

Obviously, the first thing the ski shop wants to sell you after you pick out your skis is a set of bindings. Bindings have improved so much in the past few years that there's now little difference between them, except that bindings for experts can be regulated slightly to alter the performance or release functions. This is of little concern to the skier whose basic interest is green to low expert runs.

What is significant is the DIN (Deutsche Industrie Normen, or German Industrial Standard) setting. This measures how much pressure it will take to release your boot from the binding in the event of a fall. The DIN numbers range from 1 to 10. The higher the DIN setting, the tighter the boot is locked into the binding.

Essentially, a binding whose DIN can be set between 3 and 7 can be adjusted to meet the needs of skiers whose skills range from green to low expert. Tough, rough, sturdy skiers may need a binding with a top DIN setting of 10.

Poles

Until you become a fast, aggressive skier don't throw big dollars into expensive poles. Pick an economical pair. To measure yourself for poles, turn the pole upside down, putting the grip on the ground. Grasp the tip with your hand resting on the basket. The pole is the appropriate size when your forearm is parallel to the ground.

Packages and Bargains

Discount sporting goods stores may not have the skilled personnel to help you select the equipment most suited for you, but if you're confident of what you want to buy, take a good

Herb Gordon

Need a ski pole? Whatever size you need for a rental, there will be one to meet your height and ski level.

look at the savings they can offer in their packages. Buying a "store package" of skis, boots, bindings, and poles that meet your needs can run 30 to 40 percent below the price of equipment bought separately. If the package includes last year's models the savings can easily top 50 percent.

Americans are eager pursuers of bargains, but they're notoriously weak at haggling over prices. If that's the price, then that's the price. But every ski shop salesperson is aware that some people do want to negotiate a price on precisely the gear they've selected, not the package of boots, skis, and bindings that the shop has put together, or a pair of boots alone.

So, negotiate. You could get a break. This is especially true at the end of the ski season or when last year's equipment goes on sale at the end of the summer. But, you gotta haggle.

2

Instruction and Technique

Here are two *important* sections for the "never-evers" and the "beginners." They're designed to guide the self-taught in the basic ski maneuvers that can be learned in one day on the slopes; you can use these skills to advance to a high beginner, or green-slope, level by your second day. Techniques discussed include gliding, the star turn, the sidestep, the snowplow, and the ever-important "how to fall." In the second section you'll be introduced to the snowplow turn, the stem christie, and, finally, parallel turns.

BASIC INSTRUCTION, PART 1—GETTING STARTED

The never-ever has three choices in learning how to ski:

1. Let a friend teach you.

2. Start with ski school lessons.

3. Study learn-to-ski manuals or watch the newest teaching tool, videocassettes—a couple are listed in the appendices—with guidance both for beginners and advanced skiers.

There are certain advantages and disadvantages to each choice.

1. A friend can be of tremendous help if she happens to be a certified instructor. Otherwise, remember the Gordon adage: The only thing an amateur can teach an amateur is how to be an amateur.

2. In a ski school you'll be learning from competent instructors who can teach you every level of skiing, from taking your first steps to becoming a demon expert in search of nothing but black-diamond runs for the explosive hell of it. But you'll also be sharing the instructor's time with peer-level classmates. The (expensive) solution: A private instructor.

3. You can teach yourself elemental skills if you have the patience.

This chapter will help you learn those elemental skills, but its focus is only on giving you enough knowledge that you'll be able—after a couple days on the slopes—to actually ride the lifts and ski the easy green runs.

The first do-it-yourself lessons focus on such basic techniques as how to turn around, glide forward, and get up after falling. Next comes teaching your feet the proper balance, then climbing a low hill on skis, and how to side-slip, followed by that all-important skill—the snowplow, a technique that never-evers use to both stop and make turns.

It usually takes only a day or two to learn how to control your snowplow turns. Once you can do this you've moved from the beginner to the novice level, and a novice can ski every green trail at almost every ski resort. To develop further, it makes good skiing sense to enter an advanced novice class or to take private lessons with a certified instructor.

Rentals

Always tell the attendant at the rental shop how well you ski, or whether you're a total beginner. The skilled personnel handing out the skis and boots and poles will match you to the proper ski, regardless of your size or sex. Then they'll make the appropriate DIN setting on the binding.

If renting an hourglass, the beginner should start only with the very soft models specifically designed for new and low intermediate skiers. If the rental shop has such a ski, by all means grab it. Use it from the very first day. The standard length for the hourglass is slightly shorter than that recommended for regular soft-flex skis.

Boots for beginners are softer than those for experienced skiers. Do make certain the boots you're fitted with are both snug and comfortable. A good attendant will have you put on the boots then ask you to walk around in them, wiggling your toes and lifting your heels to determine if they fit properly.

The attendant also should make certain you and your pole are matched in length for each other.

Okay, put on your boots, pick up your gear, and head for the slopes.

Lesson No. 1

No matter if you're in a circle of a half-dozen other beginners facing an instructor, learning with a buddy, or by yourself, the first requirement of skiing is the proper stance—proper for the nervous novice and the skilled expert alike. Stand with the skis slightly separated—about 6 inches apart, so that each foot is directly under a shoulder. Lean slightly forward, knees bent, until your shins are pressed against the front of your boots. Keep your center of gravity directly over your boots.

The most common error in stance is leaning the upper body too far forward with the butt sticking out over the back of the boots—a problem more common among women, because of their body shape, than among men.

Gliding Along

Next—using the poles only to help navigate—with your skis flat on the snow shuffle forward, sliding one foot at a time. Slide. Slide. Slide.

Skis flat on the snow.

Relax.

Slide. Slide. Slide.

Skis flat on the snow.

Stop. Relax. Smile.

When you're doing this properly each ski is driven straight forward in a short, gliding step. If you're stiff-legged your tips may lift and cross. Take easy glides. Don't hurry. Don't reach forward with your poles. Use them only if you need to help push yourself forward.

Glide around for a few more minutes to gain familiarity with how it feels to actually be whipping, ah, well, inching across the snow.

Teaching Your Feet

Once you've begun to learn how to glide along, stop and teach the bottom of your feet about how to position themselves for skiing.

With your eyes closed and poles held in front of you in both hands, parallel to the ground, sense when your feet are in perfect balance, equal pressure from toe to heel and from side to side. Keeping your eyes closed, lean slightly forward until your weight is on the balls of your feet and your heels are slightly elevated. Next, lean back so your weight is on your heels with your toes slightly elevated.

Repeat this several times, always with your eyes closed, until the bottoms of your feet have fully learned when you're in perfect fore-and-aft balance, weight distributed equally from toe to heel, and when the weight is on the balls of your feet, or the heels.

Next, still with your eyes closed, tilt your perfectly balanced feet slightly to the right, then to the left. In this way the bottoms of your feet will learn the feel of *edging,* or standing with the weight on one edge of the boots, then the other.

Now return to perfect balance. Voilà! Your feet have learned how to help you maintain the balance crucial to all skiing. Open those eyes. Run through the whole set of foot exercises with your eyes open.

Many experienced skiers practice the technique of reminding their feet how to know when they're in perfect balance before starting their first run of the day.

Okay, doing fine. Glide slowly forward a few more times. Ski a few steps with your weight on the balls of your feet, on the backs of your feet, tilted to one side, then the other. You'll grasp almost instantly what shift-ing the balance on your newly trained feet will do to your skis.

The Star Turn

To change direction while standing still, practice the simple star turn. Imagine that your skis are the hands of a clock, with the tips pointing toward noon and the tails as the center of the dial. Pivot one ski by lift-ing the tip but not the tail and turning the tip until it's pointing toward 2 o'clock. Place the ski firmly on the snow. Now pivot the second ski, tip up, tail down, until it's parallel with the first. Remember, use your poles for balance.

Continue this series of small pivots until you're facing in the opposite direction. Then, using the same sequence, reverse the order of rotating skis until you're again facing the direction from which you started.

The do nots:

Do not lift the whole ski off the snow.

Do not spread the tails; only the tips.

Do not put your weight on the tips, or you'll cross the tails of your skis.

The remember:

Remember that the pressure on the bottom of your feet will tell you whether you're turning with your weight on your heels, on your toes, or on your edges.

· Spend a few minutes both gliding around and making the star turn until it's time to climb a low slope for your first downhill adventure.

Climbing Hills

Skiers are carried to the summit of the trails by a variety of lifts. But they also do a lot of puffing and chugging to climb small slopes with their skis on. There are two techniques for climbing: the herringbone, which the French call the *montée en canard*, or duck walk; and the sidestep. The herringbone is used on easier slopes, the side-step on steeper pitches.

To start the herringbone, face uphill and make a wide V with your skis, the tips pointed out and the tails together. Place your poles behind you to help you push yourself up if you need to. Put your weight on the inside edges of the skis by bending your knees inward.

With your weight on one ski, raise the other and move it forward, then set it down at the same angle and put your weight on the inner edge. Lift the second ski and move it forward, again planting it with your weight on the inner edge. Go uphill step by herringbone step.

The Sidestep

For the sidestep, stand at right angles to the fall line—the direction a ball will roll—with your skis parallel and your knees inclined toward the slope so that the uphill edge of each ski is pressed into the snow. This is edging. Your feet already learned how it feels to put the weight on one edge and the other. On a slope the pressure edge is always on the uphill side.

With your weight on your downhill ski, lift the uphill ski and step up. Plant the uphill ski with your weight on the upper edge and bring the downhill ski up to and parallel with the first.

In the sidestep always, but always, keep the skis at right angles to the slope. If the skis point even slightly downhill you'll find them starting to glide downhill. If the tails point downhill you'll suddenly find yourself gliding backward toward the base.

How to Fall

Had any good falls lately? You will when skiing. Everyone does, from mighty experts to skittish novices. Not to worry. Falling on snow is much like falling on a firm mattress. Snow yields. You usually won't hurt anything, except your pride.

However, as with all ski techniques, there's only one right way to fall, and that's to fall, or sit down, sideways—dropping onto the snow, not your skis. Keep your hands upward and forward to avoid spraining a wrist or fingers.

Once you're down the problem is: How in the hell do you get back up? If the skis are tangled under you roll onto your side, or your back if it's necessary to maneuver your legs until your skis are free of your body.

If you're on a slope make doubly certain your skis are below you and at right angles to the fall line. Next, scrunch your butt close to your skis. Roll over onto your knees. Push yourself up with your poles and/or your hands, keeping your weight forward and on the uphill edge of the skis.

Remember: If your skis aren't at right angles to the fall line you'll slip or slide downhill. If your skis are too far from your body you won't be able to stand up.

It's comforting if a partner holds out a hand to help you back onto your skis, but what happens if you don't know how to get up and you're all alone on that great big mountain?

The Snowplow

Meet a new friend—the snowplow.

It's the first "moving technique" every skier must learn.

It's basic to your first turn going downhill and to stopping before crashing a) into the padded pylons holding aloft the cables that carry skiers on swaying chairs, or b) into unsuspecting friends.

To practice (while on flat ground): With your skis parallel push their tails well apart, with their tips almost together, to form a letter V with the point of the V to the front. As you push the tails apart bend your knees toward each other. You'll instantly feel the inner edges of the skis sloping inward.

When properly positioned the tips are not quite touching. But they are close together. To visualize the position, imagine that your ski tips are on the center of the dial of a clock. The tail of your right ski is at 20 minutes past the hour, and the tail of your left ski at 20 minutes to the hour.

Still on flat ground, practice several times going into a snowplow stance then returning your skis to the parallel position. They should be 4 to 6 inches apart, each ski under a shoulder, and pointed straight ahead.

Sidestepping, or using the herringbone, or—if there's a beginner area with a rope tow, using that—head up a low hill. It will be easier, for now, if you can find one that will allow you to stop on a flat surface rather than a slope. Using the star turn, face the fall line.

Hold the grips of the poles in front of you as if grasping the handlebars of a bicycle, elbows tucked in, and start gliding down. Keep your weight balanced evenly over both skis. Don't worry about what the ski poles are doing.

While moving gently, force your skis into the snowplow position. Tips close together. Knees bent in toward each other so that the inner edges of the skis are digging into the snow and the tails are spread apart. If you're properly positioned, with your weight equally over each ski, you'll come to an instant stop.

Bring the skis parallel to start gliding. Again go into the snowplow. Practice this glide-snowplow-glide-snowplow maneuver until you reach the bottom. Then head for the top of the hill again and ski-snowplow-ski-snowplow to the flat runoff.

If the snowplow doesn't function properly check to make certain your tips are close together, your knees pressed toward each other, and the tails spread apart.

If your tips are too far apart or you're not edging inward, the result is predictable: "Damn it, why don't I stop?"

If your tips are farther apart than the tails you'll discover the agonizing discomfort of doing the splits on skis. Practice getting up.

If your weight is more on one ski than the other you'll start skiing in the direction in which the weighted ski is pointed or—possibly without even knowing what you're doing—going into a snowplow turn.

Whether you learn the abovementioned techniques by yourself, with a partner, or at your first hour in ski school, smile. You're no longer a never-ever. You can control yourself skiing down an easy slope.

Side-Slipping

There will be times and places on the mountain when you'll need to side-slip to gently change your position. This requires a bit of practice. Stand at right angles to the fall line in the same stance you use for the sidestep, skis weighted to edge into the uphill side of the slope. Slowly, tilt both skis downhill at the same time until the bottoms are parallel with the snow and you're no longer edging. At this moment the skis will start sliding down the slope. To stop side-slipping, tilt the upper edges of the skis into the snow.

Lesson No. 2: Skiing the green!

BASIC INSTRUCTION, PART 2—MOVING UP

Okay, you've practiced the snowplow for stopping. Now use it to control your speed as you schuss straight down the fall line. When you begin skiing faster than you're comfortable with, push your skis into a modified snowplow, tails slightly out, tips close together but not touching. Edge lightly on the inside of each ski. When you've reduced speed, bring the skis parallel and start moving faster.

Here's a good beginner exercise for putting the snowplow into service for braking:

First—start skiing parallel, with your skis straight forward and your shoulders balanced above each ski;

Second—go into a modified snowplow with pressure on the inside edges to slow you down;

Third—return to parallel skiing to gain speed;

Fourth—use a full snowplow with strong inside edging to stop.

Fifth—repeat the first four steps. And repeat again.

How important is the position of your body? Critical! Stand erect with your shins pressing the front of your ski boots, your knees flexed, your butt tucked in, and your weight equally distributed on both skis.

The Snowplow Turn

Since you're not going to ski straight downhill forever, your next step is to learn the snowplow turn. Do this by forming a snowplow as if to slow down, then shift your weight from equally balanced between the two skis to balanced on one ski.

Put your weight on the right ski to turn left, the left ski to turn right. When turning, the ski on the outside of the turning arc is termed the *outside ski*. The ski on the inside of the arc, intelligently enough, is the *inside ski*.

Edging comes into play here. The inside edge of the outside ski—only—is dug into the snow. When you've completed the turn bring the two skis back to parallel to continue your run. Then form the skis into a snowplow again, placing your weight on the opposite ski. When the turn is complete, return to parallel. Then, of course, repeat. And repeat.

Skiing is, basically, a series of curves. Left to right to left to right. The shorter the radius of the arcs, the faster you'll travel. The wider the radius, the more gently. Practice making both short- and long-radius turns.

Continue a series of snowplow turns until you reach the bottom of a lift.

Arms and the Skier

Once you actually begin skiing—alternating between parallel while traversing the slopes and snowplow turns—you may find yourself, as we all do, with your arms flailing about, whether you're stopping, gliding, or turning.

The positions of the arms and hands are important. *Important!*

Stand with your hands in front of you—remember, you're grasping imaginary bicycle handlebars—your forearms parallel to the ground, and your elbows close to your body. Now comes the important part. *Always* keep your hands and elbows in this position when skiing.

An almost never-ending mistake, even among intermediate skiers, is letting the inside hand on a turn fall in back of the hips. This pulls you out of position with nothing more than five fingers in the wrong location. Another common problem is flapping the arms like an excited chicken flapping her wings.

Here's an exercise that will help you learn to keep your hands in front, always holding the handlebars of the bicycle.

Hold your ski poles across your body, parallel to the ground, each hand clutching both poles. Now ski slowly with the poles still held in your hands. Make a snowplow. Go into a series of snowplow turns. Snowplow to a stop. The pole "handlebars" will help keep your hands and elbows in the proper position.

Another technique for keeping your hands and arms in the proper position is to tie a piece of string in a loop as long as your hands are apart when they're in the proper position. Keep your hands in front of you. Hold your elbows in. Keep your arms far enough apart so that the loop remains taut.

For the rest of that first day on the slopes, remember what the New Yorker strolling down Fifth Avenue told a young violinist who came panting up to him and asked, nervously, "How do I get to Carnegie Hall?"

"Practice," the man replied. "Practice."

How do you learn to ski?

Why, practice.

One full day of skiing on short 140-cm skis is usually sufficient to enable most skiers to handle the easiest green runs on the mountain. In other words, you've now moved up to beginner status. It's time to go higher. And to a more appropriate length ski.

See page 28 for a chart that's an excellent guide to the appropriate length of ski for your sex, weight, age, and height.

Skis, the Second Day

If you're using the graduated-length method (GLM) to learn to ski, on your second day rent anything from a 150-cm ski (for a small person) to 170-cm (for the heavier, taller skier). Tell the fellow behind the rental counter that you're a novice and ask his advice, or—better—discuss ski length with an instructor. Most instructors are quite delighted to show off their knowledge, even if you're not taking ski school lessons. If you are, the instructor, naturally, will recommend the appropriate length.

On the other hand, if you're using parabolic skis, stay with the same length you started with.

The Stem Christie

The next step up to learning the parallel turn is sometimes referred to as a *stem christie*. Though not as widely taught as it once was, it's still an effective way to learn how to achieve linked turns.

To perform the stem christie, start from a snowplow turn. Place most of your weight on your right ski, and only light weight on the left. This will immediately put you into a left-hand curve. As you arc to the left, about halfway through the turn pull your left, or inside, ski parallel to the outside ski. You'll emerge from the turn with your skis in the parallel position.

It's not necessary to lift the inside ski off the snow, as some once believed, to start the stem christie; simply keep most of your weight on the outside ski, and light weight on the inside ski.

With your skis parallel, again go into a snowplow. This time put your weight on the left ski, shoving the left tail out. As you arc easily to the right, bring the right ski parallel to the left ski when halfway through the turn.

Continue this series of stem christies, shifting weight, bringing both skis parallel, going into a snowplow, shifting your weight to the opposite side, bringing the skis parallel when halfway through the turn, then going into the snowplow again. Do it again.

Doesn't that feel smooth and neat?

Except, just except, that if, while you were shifting weight, your hands forgot to hold onto the handlebars of the bicycle and went flailing in all directions, you probably did, too. Never mind. You know how to fall on your side. And get up.

Using the Poles

The more experienced you are as a skier, the more important your poles become. Learn how to use them from the moment you go into your first stem christie.

Before initiating the turn bend your knees, lower your center of gravity, and then, stretching your arm forward, drop the point of the pole next to the shovel of the ski that will be on the inside of the turn, and ski around it. What you've done, in effect, is to use the pole to mark the turn.

As soon as you slide into the turn, raise yourself up fully until you're ready for your next turn.

There's a sort of chant that can help you with your turns:

Down. Plant pole. Start turn. Up as you complete the turn.

Naturally, as you reach forward to plant the pole to mark the inside of the turn, you may forget that you have another hand holding another pole. The consequences of this are that your outside hand will fall in back of your outside hip, pulling you off balance. You may not fall. You will struggle to complete the turn successfully. *Keep both hands on the handlebars of the bicycle you're riding.*

What's next? You haven't gotten to Carnegie Hall yet. Practice.

Parallel Turns

Few sights are more pleasing than that of an expert skier arcing through one parallel turn after another, feet almost—but not quite—together. Often, moving from stem christie to parallel turning comes automatically with continued skiing.

As you become an advanced novice you quickly discover that, after two or three days on the slopes, the snowplow you use to initiate turns is becoming less and less pronounced. Both skis are now staying almost parallel, with your weight shifting chiefly to the outside ski as you push the tail slightly out, keeping only a light weight on the inside ski so that it's increasingly parallel to the outside ski. Behold. The parallel turn, with both skis parallel throughout the entire maneuver.

For generations skiers learning the parallel were taught to "keep the weight off the inside ski." No way. With all your weight on the outside ski the turn changes from a stem christie to a skid turn, not a smooth parallel. How do you tell them apart? In the stem christie, the outside ski usually sends up a light spray of snow while you turn. In the parallel, the skis actually glide throughout the entire turn. Always keep some of your weight on the inside ski to help convert the snow-spraying stem christie into a parallel.

Suddenly, here it is, only the end of your first couple days skiing and already you have the skills necessary to handle easy groomed runs. Now is the time to consider how much more you'll learn by taking advanced lessons in a ski school with a group of your peers, or privately. Either way, every skier, from novice to expert, always has something more to learn.

3

Off-Snow Training

Beyond learning to control how your skis move on the snow, there are two concepts that can prove exceptionally helpful to all who ski. One is understanding how hidden emotions actually affect your senses of both balance and control on the mountain. And the other is taking up some summer-fun activities that involve dynamic motion skills, which will markedly improve your skiing or the rate at which you learn.

BEFORE THE BEGINNING

As a skier I had advanced, after a couple winters, to almost feeling comfortable on any blue trail and occasionally to skiing a black trail—if it was groomed—but I still suffered from one major problem. I fell too damn much.

My falls came despite the facts that I'd taken at least a dozen lessons from good instructors, including spending that week in the French Alps skiing every day with an excellent private instructor, and often skied with friends far better than I on the slopes who occasionally dropped a hint about the proper pole plant or holding my elbows in closer. Something was wrong.

On a beautiful spring ski day—strong sun, pleasant temperature, groomed slopes—I found myself sliding into a chairlift with a skier I didn't know. For the usual mysterious reasons, the lift came to an abrupt stop halfway up. During the 10 minutes we swayed in the winter breeze without moving, we exchanged routine pleasantries, gossiped, and decided to take the same blue run from the summit together.

Edging off the lift at last, we stopped briefly to check the trail. He skied off first. I watched in envy as he carved his way swiftly and skillfully through the bumps, then shoved off to catch up with him.

He skidded to a stop and glanced over at me. I stopped in an embarrassingly familiar prone position. Once more, on our way to the bottom of the trail, I fell. As I got up from my second fall, digging the snow out of my ear and brushing the powder off my jacket, I said, "You make it look so easy."

He smiled. "Thanks. You've got good style. But could I offer a suggestion?"

"Of course."

"Let go of the mountain."

"I don't understand."

"You know what you're doing? You're holding onto the mountain with your mind. You keep falling when it's a bit steep or difficult. Let go of the mountain."

We started down. I repeated to myself what I'd just heard. "Let go," I told myself.

After we parted, I kept mulling over what he'd said—especially when I hit steep or difficult stretches.

Awareness

Suddenly, as though hit by an implosion of awareness, a satori in the richest sense of Zen—an eastern philosophy I'd studied briefly when stationed in Japan after an old war—I realized I'd been doing exactly what my companion had said. My mind clutched the mountain while I tried to free myself from it and ski. This mental holding on was a manifestation of the fear of letting go.

Be. This is probably as close to Zen as I can express the thought through western terms. Grab not for tomorrow. Do not hold onto yesterday. Release yourself. Be. The snow is snow. A mountain is a mountain. Now is now. Apprehension is one result of clinging to the impossible. There is neither behind or beyond, only now. Only here. Be. Ski.

Throughout the rest of that day, whenever and wherever I was skiing, I kept reminding myself to let go. Be.

I found that I'd begun placing my confidence where it should have been from the first time I locked my boots onto a pair of skis—in the skis.

In what they were doing. By clutching fear I could never let myself put my faith in my ability to use the ski techniques I'd been taught.

That suggestion from a friendly stranger was the first of two nonskiing lessons that turned me into a skier.

By a couple ski lessons later, far more confident than I'd ever been, I was skiing all over the mountains—but still with trepidation on the blacks. I knew I could handle them, and did, but more through determination than through skill.

Even though I'd continued to take an occasional lesson, sometimes with a mountain class, sometimes with an instructor, my skiing had reached a plateau that I couldn't seem to break out of. And then, without at first even being aware of it, I learned my second significant lesson: Balance.

It happened not on the slopes, but in a classroom. At the time I was teaching a course in The Art of Lightweight Camping at the New School in New York City. As a faculty member, I had the opportunity to take any class at this distinguished college for adults without charge. Glancing over the catalog early one evening while waiting for my own class to begin, I was intrigued by the offering of T'ai Chi Ch'uan, sometimes referred to as Chinese shadowboxing.

I enrolled. Within a few weeks I began to understand the relationship between the balance of body and that of the mind. I felt it as a down flowing, a flexible blending of the body that we'd all once accepted as young children, before we grew into stiff adults. The various positions we practiced in T'ai Chi were all an interweaving of sensitive yielding, supple movement and constant balance.

When the ski season and I finally got together on the slopes that winter, I found myself unexpectedly skiing with the same sense of balance that I'd studied in T'ai Chi classes. Down-flowing, ever-shifting balance. From the naval. Flowing easily with the snow. Not soaring. Not flying. But becoming one with motion itself.

Unbelievable. I was amazed at myself on the slopes.

Now I truly began skiing. The mountains and slopes, the moguls and the dips. Ah, it had taken so long.

A Proof

The ultimate proof that the acceptance of the now through Zen, and that the meaning of inner balance through T'ai Chi, had moved me to a level of skiing I'd never attained before came on a National Standard Race (NASTAR) course. Three or four times each season, for several years, I'd run timed NASTAR racing courses for amateurs. My usual result was the earning of a bronze racing through the flags, with an occasional silver for a particularly good run. Skiing Stowe on a weekend trip I decided to tackle NASTAR again. First run. Heart pounding. Heavy breathing. Float, I said. Carve those turns, don't fight them.

The starter waved to me. I leaped out of the starting gate. The poles flashed past.

I choked when I saw my time and heard the track announcer cry: *Gold.*

This was a goal, a level of skiing I'd long struggled to achieve, and reached only when I'd quit struggling.

A couple times ski instructors had told me to relax, to take it easy, but none had mentioned either of the two concepts that turned me into at least a low-level expert.

The first was accepting the Zen concept of mentally letting go. Of accepting how and where I was. When the mountain was steep I had clung to it with my mind. Only when I was told by a rather ordinary guru skier to let go did I do so.

The second was understanding and practicing balance on the same symbolic level taught in T'ai Chi—not fighting for balance through strength, but flowing with an inner sense of balance, flowing with the trail, letting myself adjust to balance as a willow adjusts to the wind.

The more you understand and weave these concepts into the totality of skiing, the easier it will be to learn skiing, and to become one of those someones slaloming down the slopes whom the skiers watching from the chairlifts admire.

It's not necessary, of course, to study Zen and T'ai Chi to become a skillful powder hound. Few of the dynamite skiers who cruise past you on the slopes do, though they unwittingly follow the principles of both philosophies. And, in a sense, they may have practiced the art of inner skiing that interweaves these two powerful forces.

When the yawning depths of a deep plunge on a double black diamond, or a mild plunge on a green run, concern you: Let go of the mountain. Put your faith in your skis. And, as you start sliding forward, flow with the trail, become part of the run, casual as a snowflake.

If you're curious about what you might learn from these ancient arts that would be of value in your skiing—or any other athletic skill or sport—slalom over to the nearest library or bookshop and peruse books on them.

SKIERS NEED SUMMER
Skiers are made in summer, not born in winter.

Or, to put it another way: Those who are seized with a desire to try skiing, or skiers who want to improve their skills on the snowy slopes, should take advantage of the wide range of summer activities that will not only enhance their physical condition but also improve their dynamic motion skills. Both are involved in skiing. And both apply equally to men and women, and without regard to age.

But, before discussing these two elements of off-the-slope action, let me emphasize this:

The majority of skiers, from eight-year-olds to octogenarians, are reasonably healthy. They're reasonably active. They're reasonably physically fit. And they thoroughly enjoy skiing at their own level and pace without being muscle monomaniacs or dying to ski because it's such a wild and dangerous sport.

Physical Activities
Now, let's look at physical conditioning.

Almost any sport, or workout, will do a lot to keep those muscles tuned and tingling. Pursue any that appeals to you—tennis, backpacking, handball, in-line skating, swimming, brisk walking, bicycling, rock climbing, or golf—and you've met the first requirement of conditioning.

Remember: It's important to keep those muscles working on a regular schedule and for 30 minutes, minimum, per workout, at least three times weekly. You say you'd like to add three days of exercise or an especially vigorous summer sport to your schedule only there's so much work, and you're so busy, and you don't have the time and . . . and nonsense. Take the case of Paula Zuckerman, a Manhattanite who's also a dedicated skier. Knowing there are times when she can't go for a fast 3-mile walk she makes it a practice to trudge up and down from her apartment three times daily. Of course, she only lives on the 17th floor, so it's no great strain.

Dynamic Motion Skills

Physical activities that improve your dynamic motion skills as well as strengthening muscles, heart, and lungs are the most beneficial to improving your skiing.

For example, you're rafting Idaho's roaring South Fork of the Salmon River. It's strenuous, exciting, and dynamic, but the dynamism belongs to the raft leader, not the paddlers. He tells you when and how to respond. His dynamism is in control, not yours.

Or, you swat tennis balls. Great sport. But swinging at a ball is not bouncing through moguls. Golf is fun and healthy, but it bears little resemblance to carving down the winter slopes.

There are sports, however, that both maintain or enhance your physical condition and also improve the dynamics of motion found in your skiing.

Canoe or kayak a river with rapids and rock gardens. The dynamic of doing your own paddling to navigate successfully is the same control you need on the mountain.

In the 1994 World Extreme Skiing Championships held in the Chugach Mountains of Valdez, Alaska, three or the four top finishers also were skilled kayakers.

Dean Cummings, of Santa Fe, New Mexico, who finished fourth, kayaks Class V rapids. These are so wild and dangerous they're paddled only by top experts.

Cummings says skiing and kayaking both involve the same skills, such as balance, edging, and turning. "You're mapping a line from one turn to the next, from drop to drop, even as skiers navigate the bumps on steep trails."

Dave Swanwick, of Crested Butte, Colorado, who finished first, calls kayaking and skiing "the same kind of gravity sport."

Even paddling mild white water involves the same balance and control that skiing the bumps on a high intermediate run requires. And just as the skier must constantly "read" the terrain in front of her, so, too, must the canoeist "read" the water to weave safely through the hazards.

If you have enough skill, stand up in a canoe to paddle a modest stretch of white water. You'll hardly believe the parallel to the skills necessary to whoop your way through moguls. A skier cuts into a side-slipping turn to a snow-spraying stop. Precisely the same forces are used by canoeists—in a maneuver known as an eddy turn—to whip a canoe to a halt behind a rock in fast-moving water. Standing can be done both paddling solo, or in the stern when paddling tandem.

These dynamic skills aren't really a part of rafting large, stable craft.

Bicycling utilizes dynamic motion control, most noticeably similar to skiing dynamics when you're puffing and pumping up hills and down slopes on a mountain bike.

In-line skating is a great lesson in the dynamics of motion. *Snow Country* magazine is particularly enthusiastic about it—Lisa Feinberg Densmore, former U.S. Ski Team member, wrote: "Since they simulate a carving ski better than any other device, many skiers now religiously skate during the warmer months to help stay in shape and master turning techniques. To practice, stick to pavement with a gentle pitch."

Skateboarding is superb training in dynamic motion skills of snowboarding, and also helpful to the skier.

Water-skiing involves motion and balance in somewhat the same way as snowboarding or skiing. Surfing parallels the dynamics of snowboarding. Snowboard instructors are no longer surprised that surfers pick up snowboarding almost instantaneously.

Horseback riding has earned the plaudits of ski instructors, but only when it actually involves riding at a light gallop or jumping. A casual cruise along a wooded trail on a walking horse is pleasant.

Considering the endless shapes and sizes of the exercise equipment in a modern gym, it's somewhat surprising to find that few of these machines actually engage you in the motion dynamics of skiing. One of the best is the MetroSki Simulator, a comparatively recent invention that originated in Vail. Wearing skis and boots, skiers practice carving turns on a wide, endless, sloping rug belt that rotates beneath them while they watch and try to follow the carved turns of a skilled skier actually skiing down a mountain and projected on a huge screen in front of them.

So enjoy the luxury of summer, even if it's sunbathing on the beach along with an occasional plunge into a rolling wave. But don't drift into becoming a television couch potato or a computer nerd whose virtual-reality dynamic skills wither from staring at the screen.

4

Safe Skiing

Flying off to a high-altitude ski vacation? Here's how to avoid the "altitude blahs," otherwise known as altitude sickness, which can range from feeling yucky for a few days to a serious illness requiring medical attention. As for keeping warm on the coldest of days, it's simple: Know what to eat and how to dress, and you'll be comfortable. Good skiing is more than merely taking care of yourself; it's also understanding how to rate yourself as a skier, and what this means in terms of equipment, as well as your responsibilities as a considerate skier. And, remember, your equipment needs T(ender) L(oving) C(are). So take care. Finally, included here is a list of accessories—ranging from merely helpful to the absolutely necessary.

SAFETY AND COMFORT
Altitude Sickness
Symptoms and Description
Shhhhh.

One of the least-discussed, -mentioned, or -whispered problems with skiing the great high-altitude resorts in the towering mountains is . . . the altitude blahs. Otherwise known as mountain or altitude sickness (MS), in one way or another this affects almost all skiers from lowland areas who vacation at altitudes above 7,000 feet. Generally, it sets in one or two days after we unpack our ski bags. For the most part, it's no more serious than tiring more easily and breathing somewhat more heavily than usual for the first few days after we arrive.

However, altitude sickness can also be a more serious problem. Symptoms may include any, or all, of the following: unexplained headaches not relieved by medication; a lack of appetite; sleeplessness; diarrhea; nausea; and, in some vague way resembling a hangover, not feeling especially well. Skiers may attribute their symptoms to a sudden cold, a touch of the flu, or "something I ate."

In acute cases, skiers may vomit; fainting is not uncommon. On the slopes, affected skiers may lose their sense of balance, falling frequently. There can also be changes in normal behavior patterns. A few victims will become sullen or inexplicably irritable. Extreme shortness of breath at this stage is common.

The Mountaineers, a distinguished outdoor organization in Seattle, warns: "Most people wouldn't think twice about occasional headaches, loss of appetite, or drowsiness. But at high altitudes they are not to be ignored. They are early symptoms of altitude sickness, a potentially deadly imbalance that can affect hikers, skiers, mountain climbers, and anyone traveling above 7,000 feet."

Serious altitude sickness is rare at elevations below 8,000 to 10,000 feet. But if acute problems develop at any elevation, the skier should be taken promptly to a local doctor familiar with altitude illness, or to the ski area first-aid station. If no medical help is available, The Mountaineers recommends immediate evacuation to lower altitudes.

Mountain sickness is not caused by the height of the summit where you get off the lift. This might be 9,000 or 12,000 feet. You're only at that elevation briefly. It's the base elevation—where you spend your time when you hang up your skis—that's significant.

Avoiding the Blahs

Fortunately, much can be done to prevent altitude sickness, and to ease its symptoms, even for skiers who haven't ventured higher than the top of the Empire State Building in 10 years.

One major cause of the problem, according to mountaineering authorities, is rapid change in altitude. High-speed travel can bring it on. Consider that skiers can fly from sea level in the morning to spend the night in a condo at 8,000 feet.

You can either alleviate or prevent MS by adjusting to a high altitude by steps. It helps to spend one night at a moderate altitude before going any higher. This could mean a night in Denver, or Salt Lake City, or Pocatello, or anyplace with an elevation of around 5,000 feet, before rushing off to a ski destination above 7,000 feet in the popular resort areas of Colorado, Idaho, Utah, Wyoming, or the Alps.

MS is less of a problem in Europe, however, where the usual pattern of arriving at a ski resort is to spend one day traveling from the airport by car, train, or bus to the ski area then sleep that night at resort housing usually located in the valleys. Typically, you don't actually ski the high altitudes until your second day.

Experienced mountain climbers use the slow-change-in-altitude technique to avoid MS when they venture above 10,000 feet. They increase the elevation of their campsite by only about 1,000 to 2,000 feet each night, no matter how high they may climb during the day.

After a rapid change in altitude, dehydration is the next most common cause of altitude sickness. It can also intensify a feeling of being cold while skiing.

Dehydration actually begins on your airline flight. Some authorities recommend drinking at least 4 ounces of water per hour while flying, regardless of your destination. But this is especially recommended when you'll be landing at a mountain airport—possibly even getting on the slopes by midafternoon for an hour or two of skiing.

Skiers generally recognize that even at low altitudes the body needs more fluid than usual while skiing, just as it does in the summer when you're engaged in a vigorous activity. This need for additional body fluid is sharply increased if the skiing takes place above 7,000 feet. At low altitudes, the normal intake of fluid for an average, active male is about 2 to 3 quarts daily (slightly less for a female). At high altitudes in winter, the same active man requires from 3 to 5 quarts daily.

One way to avoid dehydration for both men and women is to drink a minimum of 4 full cups of water a day, in addition to all other liquid intake. When we're skiing the altitudes we've found a delicious way to increase liquid intake is to start each lunch and dinner with soup.

Dr. Judith Brown, a professor at the University of Minnesota School of Public Health, says that even under normal conditions the average person doesn't drink enough liquid. To maintain body fluid levels at high altitudes she recommends drinking water rather than other liquids because it's rapidly absorbed by the body.

"The more sugar something has, the more slowly it is absorbed. Fruit juice by itself is too sweet, so I dilute it half and half. Soda is bad because of the sugar—not only because it's more slowly absorbed, but also because you need fluid to digest sugar. So sugar actually causes you to lose fluid. Nothing makes you thirstier than a Coke."

Caffeine is a mild diuretic and can increase water loss, says Dr. Brown. There's no particular need to avoid coffee or tea, however; just don't rely on them for increasing your fluid consumption.

Before they suffer from such early signs of altitude dehydration as nausea, weakness, and lack of concentration, climbers have a simple technique for determining whether or not they're getting enough liquid: the appearance of their urine. A very light color generally indicates good liquid intake. A dark color is considered a warning they must increase intake of fluids.

Tips

Here are some additional notes on avoiding the altitude blahs:

Alcohol depresses respiration—critical for acclimatization—especially during sleep. Drink water or pure juice, not alcohol, on your flight out. After you arrive, minimize or avoid the convivial drinking at the noisy bar, the wine with dinner, or the friendly nightcap for your first two or three days—until you adjust fully to the altitude.

Unless approved by a doctor familiar with altitude complications, sleeping pills, sedatives, or tranquilizers should be avoided as cures for sleeplessness or mild attacks of the blahs. Like alcohol, they depress respiration; this can exacerbate high-elevation illness.

Smokers, if they can, should drop the habit when skiing. Smoking affects the intake of oxygen and this, in turn, can bring on MS.

Dr. Fred T. Darvill Jr., author of *Moutaineering Medicine*, recommends a "high carbohydrate intake" before you start a trip to the mountains, as well as for the first few days after you arrive, to ease your passage into a soaring ski experience. Dr. Stephen Bezruchka, author of *Altitude Illness*, also suggests "a low-fat, low-salt, and high-carbohydrate diet." However, he calls a good appetite a "sign of acclimatization, so eat what appeals to you. The widely touted high-energy foods may not be palatable up high. Thin people may welcome some fat in the diet to help keep insulation from melting away."

Jet lag is only a minor cause of mountain sickness, but if it's a problem try the "Feast-Fast Jet Lag Diet." This was developed at a U.S. Department of Energy lab. For information, send a self-addressed stamped envelope to Argonne National Laboratory, 9700 South Cass Avenue, Argonne, IL 60439.

Racing off to the mountains the first day to ski your butt off can push even a healthy athlete into the blahs, a disease that respects neither ego nor muscles. Take it easy for the first two or three days on those high slopes, and relax at night with a bit of extra sleep. In other words, remember the three basic rules for avoiding altitude problems:

Acclimate!

Acclimate!

Acclimate!

Your ski holiday will be a helluva lot more fun.

Ski Area Responsibility

It is, frankly, a foolishness akin to an ostrich hiding its head in a snow-bank for any high-altitude resort not to help skiers—in some discreet way, of course—recognize that the elevation may cause difficulties. I found it a pleasant surprise to read skier-friendly advice about altitude problems and how to avoid them altogether when I was staying at the Vail Athletic Club Hotel while skiing Vail—base elevation 8,200 feet.

Many major western ski areas have base elevations above 7,000 feet. One of the few exceptions is Sun Valley. When Averell Harriman, then president of the Union Pacific Railroad, wanted to build the ski resort in the pre–air travel depression of the 1930s to spur business, he brought over an old European ski buddy, Count Felix Schaffgotsch of Austria, to help find a location.

Harriman told the count he had only one requirement: The resort must be reachable by the Union Pacific. The count added a second requirement. He told Harriman, "A ski resort shouldn't be over 6,000 feet because [higher altitude] affects too many people."

One after another the count toured and rejected snowy mountains—some of which are today famed winter playgrounds—because of their base elevations. He finally visited Ketchum, a sleepy mountain town. He checked the altitude in front of the Pioneer Saloon, later Ernest Hemingway's favorite mountain watering hole. It was 5,750 feet. He wired Harriman that he'd found the perfect place: towering mountains, heavy snows, and a reasonable base altitude.

Sun Valley opened in 1936.

Frostbite

The cold, not the altitude, is the cause of frostbite. When outdoors, especially on windy days for prolonged periods, exposed skin may suffer mild "frostnip" or the more dangerous "frostbite" without any sense of pain. The first sign of trouble is white skin, especially around the face and ears. Wise skiers check each other occasionally for the telltale warnings on cold, cold days.

To treat frostnip rewarm the skin by covering it with a warm hand, or blowing on it gently; then cover the exposed skin and head off immediately to a warm area. When the skin is fully rewarmed it may itch, but there will be no permanent damage. However, the affected area should be examined promptly by first-aid attendants at the ski area.

In frostbite, a deeper layer of skin actually freezes into ice crystals. The frozen skin is white and hard, but there's still no pain. It's imperative that the victim of frostbite get medical assistance as swiftly as possible. Never rub or massage the frozen skin, since this may tear the affected cells, causing permanent skin damage. Protect the frozen skin by covering it with cloth—never any ointment or heat—until proper medical help can be obtained.

Even under proper treatment, when frostbitten skin is rewarmed the tissues swell and the pain is brutal. The affected skin often becomes covered with blood-filled blisters, which can result in gangrene.

Hypothermia

Hypothermia is rare on the ski slopes. It's most apt to occur on long backcountry ski or snowshoe trips and can develop even in temperatures well above freezing. The victim is often a thin person who becomes chilled, physically exhausted, and wet. This results in a dangerous drop in core-body temperature, manifested by a rapid increase in pulse and respiration and a loss of physical control. This is more a matter of the body feeling as though it is cold, than the actual temperature, though some experts say the core temperature may register a couple of degrees below normal, but the skin is actually much colder because of sluggish circulation.

In hypothermia's first stage, falling becomes frequent. Sometimes the victim is unable to stand without help. Near the end of this stage, the body begins to feel cold to the touch, pulse and respirations slow, and shivering decreases or disappears.

The next stage, occurring when the core temperature drops to about 88 degrees, is confusion and defective thinking. Without treatment there's a loss of consciousness, and an irregular heartbeat develops. Death occurs when the core temperature drops to about 81 degrees.

There's only one treatment: immediately warming the victim's torso as quickly as possible. "Under no circumstances," says Dr. Darvill, "should the extremities be treated until the torso is warmed. To do so will simply further lower the body's temperature."

The best choice, if available, is to rewarm in water of between 104 and 112 degrees. The patient can also be sandwiched between two warm skiers, or wrapped with warm stones. Heat must be maintained until the shivering ceases. Offer warm liquids but avoid alcohol or caffeinated drinks.

On long backcountry trips, prevention is safer than treatment. Experienced winter mountaineers carry extra food and eat frequently, especially proteins rich in fat, which produce slow-burning calories. If the weather deteriorates they set up a protected campsite, build a fire, and just hunker down until it's safe to get up and get going again.

KEEPING WARM
Light clouds skidded across the sky. It was a cold, cold day to sit in a sway-ing chairlift for the 10-minute ride to the summit. Some skiers hunkered down in the chairs, trying to shrink inside their clothing and keep from turning into frozen statues. Others, however, appeared quite at ease—if not completely comfortable—skiing on a day when the base lodge was crowded with skiers who, moaning about how brutal it was outside, watched from the comfort of tables by the windows or crowded onto stools at the bar.

Well, it was winter. And when the storm came along to deliver enough snow to keep the trails blanketed until spring, it was only an expected part of the ski scene, even as are those magnificent days when the sun is bright, the wind is calm, and skiers peel off extra clothing to keep from sweating.

Those who dislike cold may assume skiers enjoy it. We don't. But there are a number of steps that can be taken to keep comfortable, if not always toasty warm, when the mercury plunges to indecent lows.

Food

First, turn up your own body furnace. This is done with calories, lots of fat and juicy calories. Calories provide the fuel your body needs to maintain its heating system.

Between the activity level of skiing and the body's need for heating energy in cold weather, skiers burn up calories at an astonishing rate. To try to maintain comfort on the slopes by following a low-activity, low-calorie, hold-down-the-fat-and-avoid-the-sugar diet is precisely wrong. Add calories—especially fats, the most concentrated form of food energy. Long after your body has digested the sugars and carbohydrates for quick energy, the fat will still be providing fuel for all-day warmth. Fat has almost twice the calories per gram of any other nutrient, and calories are heat. At least one-third of the calories in a cold-weather diet should come from fat.

Skiers aware of the need for fats for body warmth often carry small sticks of sausage to chew on during the ride up on especially cold days, thus maintaining the body's fuel level. Nibbling sausages is also popular among winter mountaineers who backpack on snowshoes, climb icy cliffs, or pitch their tents protected by a snowbank. Chewing chunks of blubber between meals is a winter-survival technique the Inuit have practiced for centuries.

Vegetarians reluctant to turn to fat-rich proteins still can slather on butter, eat cheese, and drink whole milk to put fat in their diets. And all of us can gulp down those rich, tasty, sumptuous desserts we only fantasize about at home. We'll burn up every calorie the next day.

Protein is the fuel for tissue growth and critical for all body processes. The body doesn't burn protein for energy until all fat reserves are used up. Proteins should make up from 10 to 20 percent of daily calories.

Even on the coldest days, the body sweats. At high altitudes, dry air removes body moisture via respiration. Water is a temperature regulator, so the lost fluid must be replaced—if for no other reason than to increase your comfort. In addition to normal fluid consumption, drink extra water daily.

All caffeinated fluids, including coffee, tea, and Coke, as well as those containing alcohol, are diuretics, speeding the loss of body fluid. While aromatic herbal teas don't contain caffeine, be certain you're not allergic to the herb in the tea you drink.

Advocates of leave-out-the-salt diets must also be aware that, since salt helps the body retain fluids, it's important to return to normal salt use on those icy winter days—unless, of course, minimizing salt has been recommended by your doctor for genuine medical reasons.

Skin Care

The body is normally covered with a natural oil. This invisible layer helps the cells retain moisture and this, in turn, helps the body stay warmer. If you insist on showering, or bathing, every day, do so as soon as you come off the mountain, so that the body oils washed off by the soap and water will build up again overnight. When the weather is brutal, it's better, if you don't mind, to bathe every second or third day. If you're fussy, splash on a lovely scent—on your clothing, not your skin. For the elegant gentleman who shaves daily, this also should be done in the evening, not in the morning.

Keep your shower or bath short and wash only with mild soap. If you still suffer from dry skin, apply a moisturizing lotion before stepping out of the hot, moist bathroom.

Dressing Warmly

Layers

Of course, converting to a long-energy, cold-weather diet is only the foundation of keeping warm. Next comes clothing.

Dress in layers. Two lighter garments that trap air between them hold in more warmth than a single thick one. The two garments also have another advantage: When you get too warm, you can take one of them off.

Start the layering with long underwear. The new polypropylene fabrics are excellent, wicking moisture away from the body yet holding in the heat.

Warning: Cheap "winter" underwear made of cotton is an absolute no-no, no matter how fancy the weave. And wool both is uncomfortable and doesn't release body moisture as well as polypro fabrics do.

On particularly icy days, some skiers wear light silk underwear next to the skin and the long johns on top of them.

Slip on only top-quality ski socks. These may be made from anything from wool to polypro fabrics, though I recommend the latter. They should be moderately snug, but never, never tight. Tight socks restrict the flow of blood to the feet, thus compounding the problem of frozen tootsies inside heavy ski boots. If you have a problem with sweaty feet, it may help keep them dry to rub them with an antiperspirant before putting on your socks in the morning.

Many skiers forget that the inner ski-boot lining may become damp. Every night place your boots in a warm place to facilitate drying, or—if snow got inside the boot—loosen or remove the liner and let it dry out.

It helps feet keep warm if tight boots are popped loose on the ride to the summit.

Hint: On a particularly cold day, when you head into the base lodge slip into a bathroom that has an electric hand and face drier. Remove your frozen boots and heat them under the drier.

Outerwear

Outerwear usually consists of a warm turtleneck and the ski outfit itself. A two-piece garment, pants and jacket, is superior to a single-piece. The single-suit may look sleek, and certainly is, but it's either all on or all off. On the other hand, a two-piece outfit with a jacket that consists of a water-resistant outer layer and a removable inner liner (which may be kept on in cold spells or taken off on warm days) is the more adaptable. Bib-style pants are warmer than regular ski pants. If you do wear regular pants, hold them up with suspenders, not a belt.

If the weather is exceptionally cold, add an inner fleecy polyester or down-filled vest or sweater.

Ski jackets, as well as most winter outdoor garments, are filled with either down or man-made fibers. Top-quality down is the warmest filling, ounce for ounce, known. It's expensive, and worth it.

However, there's only one—only one—way to evaluate the quality of the down in any garment: its "fill" capacity. According to federal standards, down with up to 20 percent feathers can still be labeled "down." With a higher percentage of feathers, the label must specify "down and feather fill."

Fill capacity is the cubic inches an ounce of down will fill. Excellent-quality down has a fill capacity of no less than 550. In other words, an ounce will expand to fill 550 cubic inches. Superior down has a fill capacity of 600 to 700.

To avoid telling consumers the fill capacity, many outfitters, some with highly prestigious names, loudly and proudly proclaim that their garments are filled with "Prime" down, or "Southern Goose" down, names full of sound and fury that signify nothing more than that the garment is probably overpriced. All quality down products have a tag or marker specifying the fill capacity. *If the fill capacity isn't listed, a smart shopper will immediately go elsewhere.*

Man-made fibers range from very good to excellent. The best have a comparative fill capacity of 400 to 500, are superior to garments marked "down and feather," and are less costly.

All the man-made fibers used as fill in outerwear and sleeping bags do have one characteristic superior to down. When down gets wet, it flattens into a soggy nothing. When man-made fibers get wet they can be wrung out and still maintain their loft.

Eventually, all garments must be cleaned. All man-made fibers can be dry-cleaned. However, unless a dry cleaner uses the special solution that does not harm down—a solution prohibited in many cities because it's highly inflammable—a down garment should be washed only with the special down soap sold at outing goods stores or a pure, mild soap. It should never be washed with detergent.

Either was by hand or with the washing machine set for warm—never hot—on the delicate cycle. Immerse the garment and squeeze out all the air before washing.

Dry only at a mild temperature, intended for delicate fabrics, in a drier. Toss in a tennis shoe during the drying cycle. The tumbling shoe will help break up clots of down. Down garments hung out to dry may require a couple days to regain their loft.

While outer ski clothing fabrics are generally highly resistant to water, this resistance will wear off with time. It can be restored by spraying an older garment with a water-repellent spray, such as Scotch-Guard.

Occasionally, even in midwinter, regardless of where you ski, snowflakes fall as rain. Since skiing with an umbrella is awkward, and wearing a raincoat on the slopes is difficult, a handy way to keep dry can be found in any grocery store: a large plastic garbage bag. Cut a hole in the bottom big enough to slide your head through, cut out armholes on either side, and let 'er rain. When the rain stops, roll up the bag and stuff it into a jacket pocket.

Garments whose zippers or buttons are covered by flaps are more effective in keeping out the arctic blasts than those without the flaps.

Gloves and Caps and Gaiters

On the coldest of days, wear a neck gaiter or face mask. If the wind blows, you can pull up the gaiter to cover your face. It will hold in the heat better than a suede face mask. If the weather turns warm, I gratefully pull off my polypro neck gaiter and stuff in inside my ski jacket. Ankle gaiters are helpful in keeping snow spray from splashing inside boot tops exposed by tight-fitting ski pants.

Since up to 50 percent of body heat is lost through the head alone, only a truly warm cap that can be pulled down to cover the ears and forehead is worthy to put on a skier's head. The new man-made fabrics that resist wind and water but permit sweat to escape are the most comfortable. When it's a brutal day, make certain that the front of the cap actually is tucked under the top of your goggles.

Only quality gloves, never the cheap look-like-they're-expensive kind, truly protect your hands. After all, they're in the cold all day. It helps if the outer fabric is water resistant, as is, for instance, Gore-Tex. Fingered gloves are not as warm as mittens. For more comfort, you always can slip on a pair of silk inner gloves with either gloves or mittens.

Frigid hands, feet, or both can be warmed almost instantly using the new, small packages of warming chemicals sold at every ski shop. The heat will last some four to six hours, though its level drops after the first three.

Fillers and Fibers

Here's a rundown of the most common synthetics used in winter and outdoor clothing:

Thinsulate: A polyester blend made by 3M that consists of 35 percent polyester and 65 percent olefin. It's spun into a thin insulation for use in hats, gloves, and outerwear.

Capilene: A polyester fiber from the Patagonia company. It wicks moisture from the skin to the surface, where it evaporates. It's used in underwear, garment linings, and socks.

Thermolite: A Dacron polyester made by DuPont that's used as lightweight insulation in gloves, footwear, and outerwear.

Entrant: An elastic coating of waterproof polyurethane that breathes through microscopic holes that allow body moisture to escape but block rain from penetrating. It's used chiefly in rain gear and to waterproof gloves.

Polartec: A name for various fabrics made of polyester fleece by Maiden Mills. Polartec is made in several weights of polyester pile, a double-sided microfiber, and Lycra stretch.

Synchilla: What Patagonia calls its Polartec filling.

Gore-Tex: The most widely known insulation laminated to outer fabrics. It permits body moisture to escape through microscopic holes that also prevent rain from entering.

Hollofil: A hollow fiber made of Dacron polyester for lower-priced sleeping bags and outer garments. Hollofil II is the premium brand. It resists flattening better than plain Hollofil.

Microloft: A synthetic fiber made of filaments thinner than human hair. It's used in gloves, outerwear, and sleeping bags.

Microfiber: A fine, tightly woven fiber that breathes while protecting against cold; it's called, among other names, Super Microft and Versatech.

Polypropylene: Derived from petroleum, this is a strong, paraffin-based fiber that wicks moisture away from the body. It's widely used in underwear and garments worn next to the skin.

Primaloft: Micropolyester fibers interwoven into a lightweight alternative to down. It's used in sleeping bags and outerwear.

ABILITY AND RESPONSIBILITY

Do you know your ability on skis?

Downgrade yourself and you might never face those challenges that could make your skiing a more exciting and rewarding experience. To overrate yourself, on the other hand—as too many of us are inclined to do—will, sooner or later, get you into trouble, usually trying to keep up with some friends on a black diamond covered with moguls and cruddy snow with a storm whirling in.

Not actually knowing how you rate as a skier also can prove a mistake when you're buying, or renting, skis and boots. For a low intermediate to buy a hot-looking ski for experts won't make an expert out of him. It will make his skiing more difficult. An expert ski doesn't forgive a mistake. The softer-flex ski for a low intermediate does.

There are several ways to evaluate your own ability on the slopes. One is to take lessons. A skilled instructor will need perhaps 30 seconds to evaluate your ability as you ski down the practice slopes.

Another is to test yourself in an amateur National Standard Race (NASTAR); these are offered by most ski areas. You pit yourself only against a top expert, not other skiers.

Here's how NASTAR works: A ski racecourse, with all the paraphernalia—flags, poles, a starting platform, and an electronic timer—is set up on nothing more challenging than an intermediate run. An expert skier whose skill level has been rated at a national meeting of NASTAR pacesetters will run the course twice. His best time becomes the standard for that course on that particular day.

When you race the course, your time, with a handicap based on your age and sex factored in, is matched only against the expert's, not those of other skiers.

If the pacesetter's time is, by way of example, 35.6 seconds, and yours is 45.6, but you have a 10-second handicap, you'd "equal" the pacesetter's time and win a gold medal.

You could also win a silver, a bronze, or nothing but a smile and an awareness of how well you've learned to ski.

A recommendation: If you enter a NASTAR race, it's tremendously helpful to take the approximately one-hour-long NASTAR racing school that's usually offered on days when races are scheduled.

Ratings

Another way to evaluate your ability is against a definition of skill levels.

Here's one widely used:

Level 1: Total beginner. May or may not have ever put on skis before.

Level 2: Has skied a few times. Can make wedge or snowplow turns and stop fairly easily.

Level 3: Can get on and off a chairlift with no problems. Can link wedge turns on gentle green slopes and stop when desired.

Level 4: Has begun to experience the speed and excitement of skiing. Can make linked stem turns on green slopes and occasionally ventures out to easier blues.

Level 5: Skis all green runs comfortably. Has some difficulty controlling speed and making turns on steeper blues. Has difficulty keeping the upper body facing downhill; often overrotates in turns. Uses poles for balance rather than timing.

Level 6: Skis blue and green terrain exclusively. Can control speed effectively on moderately difficult blues but cannot always link turns. Has difficulty in powder snow deeper than 3 inches. Falls often in difficult snow.

Level 7: Occasionally skis black terrain, big bumps, or difficult snow but is most comfortable skiing groomed blues and easier blacks at moderate speed with linked parallel turns. Skis small bumps, but cautiously, with occasional lapses in balance. Has frequent balance problems in difficult snow and harder terrain.

Level 8: Skis blue terrain with total confidence and stability. Skis moderately sized, widely spaced bumps and basic expert runs with control at moderate speeds. Skis big, difficult bumps at controlled speeds and can link four to six turns before suffering a lapse in balance. Has trouble making linked turns in difficult snow.

Level 9: Looks and skis like a Level-10 skier on all groomed terrain but has occasional lapses in balance in big bumps and difficult snow conditions, such as crud or deep, wet snow.

Level 10: Skis all terrain with absolute confidence, rock-solid stability, and balance. Can ski a variety of lines through difficult bumps—over the tops, through the troughs—and cruise open steeps at high speed. Can ski all snow conditions equally well.

Here's another popular evaluation system, often used by ski instructors:

Never-Ever: A total beginner who may or may not have ever put on skis before. Recommended skiing: The flat surface in front of the base lodge where the ski school meets.

Beginner: Can make a snowplow or wedge turn and usually stops when desired. Recommended skiing: the greens, easy blues—and more lessons.

Low Intermediate: Is beginning to link parallel turns and can actually ski and stop with only minor problems. Recommended skiing: Green and blue trails. Should remember to take an occasional lesson, either private or with a peer group, to keep improving.

Intermediate: Can ski parallel on blue runs; has some ability to handle moguls, crud, or heavy snow; on a steep pitch, though, does more sideslipping than skiing. Stays basically with the blues, but challenges the blacks if they're wide and groomed. Will often stay at this level for years in the foolish belief that lessons are only for beginners.

Advanced Intermediate or Low Expert: Now you're getting pretty good. Can ski carved turns on almost any smooth surface, even a black. Run into problems, however, on steep runs pockmarked with moguls or covered with heavy snow or crud, or on double black diamonds. Recommended skiing: Use your own judgment. Lessons? Use your own judgment.

Expert: Hey, move over. Here she comes. Any run. Any time. Any condition. With proper training, gives lessons.

The Skier's Responsibility

Safety on the mountain is a twofold responsibility: that of the individual skier or snowboarder, no matter his level of ability, and that of the ski resort. To inform skiers of their own obligations on the mountain, the National Ski Areas Association has renamed and revised the original "Skier's Responsibility Code." It's now known as "Your Responsibility Code." It says:

1. Always stay in control and be able to stop or avoid other people or objects.

2. People ahead of you have the right of way. It is your responsibility to avoid them.

3. You must not stop where you obstruct a trail or are not visible from above.

4. Whenever starting downhill or merging into a trail, look uphill and yield to others.

5. Always use devices to help prevent runaway equipment.

6. Observe all posted signs and warnings. Keep off closed trails and out of closed areas.

7. Prior to using any lift, you must have the knowledge and ability to load, ride, and unload safely.

Similar rules of mountain etiquette and skier responsibility are also observed on the world ski scene, no matter where you head for the excitement of the slopes. Here, for example, are the 10 rules that Austria asks its skiers to observe:

1. Keep equipment in good condition.

2. Do not endanger others or destroy property.

3. Ski in control; keep weather and terrain in mind.

4. It's the uphill skier's responsibility to avoid the skier below him. Give other skiers a good, safe margin.

5. After stopping, look around before starting again.

6. Get up quickly after a fall and do not stop on blind spots on the trails.

7. If you walk up a slope, keep to the edge of the run.

8. Obey all signs and markers.

9. You are obliged to help injured skiers. Protect them from further risk and get first aid.

10. If you are in a skiing accident you are required to furnish identification. (*Note:* Visitors are expected to produce their passport and/or visa. Other identification, such as an international driver's license, is considered only temporary until the official documents are produced.)

Who Pays the Piper?

If a skier runs into serious difficulty skiing beyond an area's boundaries, someone will be along to help him. In the United States, this task usually falls to a resort's ski patrol or, if he's waaaay over there, to a trained mountain rescue unit. No matter that he got in trouble through his own idiocy; he will be rescued. There's growing sentiment, however, to charge the person rescued for the cost. And it's not unusual in the wild regions of western mountains for the skier to find himself charged with what amounts to trespassing and fined by the local courts. Insurance may cover injuries, but it doesn't cover fines.

In Europe, there's no question about who pays the piper. If you skid in a spray of snow into trouble outside the area, you do. It could prove a deadly shock to a skier's pocketbook to discover that the helicopter sent to pluck him from the side of the mountain costs hundreds of dollars.

Ski areas mark their boundaries to indicate where their responsibility ends and to warn skiers that the terrain outside their control is not patrolled, is not maintained, and may contain very dangerous and unseen hazards.

I've been at areas where skiers foolishly chose to challenge the closed boundaries. If some enjoyed the experience and bragged about it, I'm also aware of two who didn't. One was a skier rescued after 24 hours lying in a deep hollow with a broken leg. He was spotted by a helicopter. The frozen body of the other was found by a search party two days after he disappeared skiing beyond the boundaries.

Resort Responsibility

It's standard practice in the United States to print, on the back of each lift ticket, a release stating that the skier accepts and voluntarily assumes the risks of injury, and, in turn, releases the resort from all liability while he's skiing. Is this binding?

In a case in Wisconsin, the courts upheld the validity of such a release in barring the parents of an 11-year-old girl from suing a resort when she died after crashing into the unprotected steel legs of a lift tower. The parents appealed on the grounds the resort should have padded the tower—customary at most ski areas. The appeal was denied.

In Vermont, the courts held that, while skiers assume risks, the ski resorts themselves must also exercise due care in protecting skiers. That ruling came after a skier crashed into an unpadded steel pole and suffered permanent injuries. The resort paid.

Certainly skiers, like participants in all sports in which there's an inherent risk of injury, do accept this fact when they slip into their skis. But at the same time, it's clear that resort owners also have a responsibility to skiers from known dangers.

What's the bottom line? Between skiers becoming increasingly aware of their own responsibilities, and the efforts of resorts to prevent problems that are within their ability to control, skiing at resorts has never been safer.

TLC FOR SKI GEAR

You're excited about your first ski trip of the season. You've checked everything. It's all there. Even the spanking-new, warm, waterproof gloves you've needed for two years.

But before you snap on those skis for your first run, have you calibrated yet? Yes, calibrated, not celebrated.

A few skiers—not many, but a few—somehow have the impression that skis, boots, and bindings are the only objects made by man that are perfect and last forever. They never need adjusting. Maybe edge sharpening, but that's all.

Wroooong!

Bindings

Only in the past few decades has the ski industry developed bindings that actually release the foot in a slow, twisting fall as well as in a high-speed impact. But the finest bindings must still be checked for proper setting from time to time.

So, what do you do to keep your bindings working properly? *Have them cleaned and calibrated for your weight and ability by an expert at the start of each season.* Calibrating is simplicity itself. Take the skis into a well-equipped, responsible ski shop and recite the following incantation: "I would like to have my bindings cleaned and calibrated."

It takes but a few minutes. The ski is locked into a special vise. The mechanic snaps your boot into the binding, then inserts a gadget that looks like a skeletal foot with a gauge attached, and twists. He does this three times to get an average pressure setting.

He then takes a reading of the DIN force required by your particular binding to release the boot properly for you, taking into account the length of your boot (because this affects the leverage your ski can apply to your leg in a fall) as well as your age, sex, weight, and skill level, and adjusts the binding settings in both the toe and heel pieces, if necessary.

It often is.

On the other hand, don't accept a binding check if the technician simply locks your boots into the bindings and tests release pressure by banging them with his hand. A calibrated check is accurate. The guy's hand is not.

A good technician should make note of the wear on your boots' heels and toes when calibrating bindings, and advise you if they're too worn for the bindings to function properly. If so, you have three options: 1) buy new boots, 2) have new toe and heel tips attached to your boots, or 3) understand, and accept, a possible source of future problems.

It will save scruff and wear on your heel and toe tips if you always don après-ski boots or shoes and carry your boots when tromping across the parking lot from your car to the base lodge.

Of course, if your bindings aren't properly calibrated and don't release when they should, or do release when they shouldn't, you may have the dubious pleasure of riding down the hill on a stretcher toboggan pulled by a skilled member of the National Ski Patrol. Your friends can wave down at you as you glide by on your way into the first-aid station.

Skis

How sharp and smooth are your edges? You can tell with a fingernail. Brush your nail lightly across the edge. If the edge is sharp, a slight amount of your nail will peel off.

Run your fingers up and down the edges. Do you feel rough spots? Ever tumble head-over-moguls when your edges got caught? Having rough edges is one reason you fell.

You can keep your edges reasonably sharp and remove minor burrs in a minute using a special edge file sold by ski shops. Every well-equipped ski shop can also quickly and professionally sharpen the edges of your skis, as well as remove minor gouges on the base, with a high-speed dry sand belt. If you didn't have your edges sharpened and bases smoothed after your final run last spring, do so before your first run this winter.

It's also advisable to have the ski shop sharpen your edges and remove minor scratches on your ski bottoms after every week to 10 days of skiing and, of course, immediately in the event of damage to the edges or gouges on the base.

Hot-waxing at the time the shop takes care of other problems is optional but highly recommended.

Deep cuts or scratches on a ski bottom could mean trouble. Moisture seeping in through a cut can damage the interior of a ski. Get it patched.

I highly recommend a major tune-up after every several weeks of skiing. This includes edge sharpening on a wet sand belt, filling gouges on the bottoms of the skis, a hot-wax job, and, of course, having the bindings calibrated.

While skiing, give your barrel staves a quickie hand-wax job every couple days with any of the general-purpose sprays or waxes, available in ski shops. The best are fluorocarbon waxes, which work in almost every snow condition, from ice to warm mush.

It's using common sense to protect skis before putting them away for the season. Sharpen the edges. Clean the bindings. Repair tears in the base. Oil them lightly and store them in a dark, cool corner of the basement.

Herb Gordon

Boot and Ski Care

Usually, the only care your boots need is a nightly airing and drying. Some skiers pull the inner lining loose every evening for better airing. Others won't touch the lining unless it's soaked from snow getting inside the top of the boot.

One problem with older boots is the interior padding. Eventually, it flattens. This may create a problem because the boots no longer can be tightened adequately, or are physically uncomfortable to wear.

You can buy new linings for almost all boots. Ski shops frown on this for obvious dollar reasons and a) seldom tell customers they can buy new linings, and b) seldom recommend them—though they are skilled at recommending new boots.

Skiers who carry their skis on a car rack should protect the delicate bindings from salt spray, which comes from the salt used to keep winter highways open. Either carry the skis in a ski bag or wrap the bindings in a ski gaiter.

Skis should be placed in a car rack with the tips pointed backward to keep them from flapping at high speeds.

When you put your skis away for the day you should first dry them and wipe down the edges with a lightly oiled cloth. Damp edges can develop rust, even overnight.

It's especially important to clean and wipe the edges with that lightly oiled rag before your skis are stashed in a cool, dry basement for the season. Skis should be stored upright. Individually. They should not be stored with the brakes holding them together like two impassioned lovers. This could affect the camber of those expensive barrel staves.

Hey, listen. Skiing with grace and rhythm for all to admire is tough enough when everything is super. So keep your equipment in top shape.

Protecting Your Skis

No pair of skis at any ski area in the world is immune from the highly contagious disease called: OH, SHIT. SOMEONE STOLE MY SKIS.

The only prevention is locking them.

Many skiers have the odd idea that if they separate their skis in the racks they won't disappear. They will and they do if they're either new skis, or skis with new and valuable bindings, when the pros are at work. Here's why:

The average theft takes place within a few minutes from the time the hapless victim has been singled out by the thief for the skis she's carrying over her shoulder as she heads for the base lodge. He knows that once the chosen victim has stacked her skis and tromped inside it will be several minutes, at least, before she returns. Ergo. Grab and disappear, skis and thief.

The thief has already outwitted the skier who didn't lock up her skis. If she separated her pair, he simply spotted where the two skies were placed.

My twin daughters and I discovered the hard, expensive way how fast the pros operate. The two young ladies had each gotten sparkling new skis and we were off for their first day on the slopes with them. Around mid-morning we decided to duck into the lodge for a hot drink. We each locked our skis. We thought. But within minutes after walking into the base lodge, one of the twins said, "Dad. Look!" She was holding her lock in her hand. "I forgot."

"Well," I said. "Let's lock them up."

It had only been a few minutes since we'd stacked our skis. But by the time we walked back to where they were, one pair wasn't.

A variety of locks are available in ski shops. The most popular model is a cable from 2 to 3 feet long with a male and a female end. The cable can be looped through two pairs of skis and around a post with the male

Even an inexpensive dial lock is all it takes to deter theives.

Herb Gordon

end locked inside the female. The most intelligent lock is one that uses a dial for opening and closing, not a key: Keys do get lost. However, almost any cable lock, cheap or expensive, will deter a thief. It's not smart for him to take out a pair of chain cutters to work the skis free. Someone might start screaming.

ACCESSORIES

Warning: Do you *really* need it? (Of course. Why do you think I bought it?) Here's a list of accessories that range from the helpful to the necessary.

1. Goggles. The double-lens ski goggles resist steaming up inside better than the single-lens kind. Most important, especially at high altitudes, according to Dr. Barry Chaiken, a New York ophthalmologist who also happens to be an avid skier, is to wear only those that filter out damaging ultraviolet A and B rays. A lens coating—technically known as UV400—is generally but not always applied to ski goggles today. It blocks more than 99 percent of the UVA and UVB rays. Make certain your goggles have this coating.

You can buy goggles ground to your eyeglass prescription, if necessary. However, if you already have prescription sunglasses you might consider, as I do, wearing goggles with a clear lens over them.

Ski goggles range in price and style to fit both modest and elaborate budgets. All modern ski goggles are made with lenses which protect the eye against damage from ultraviolet rays.

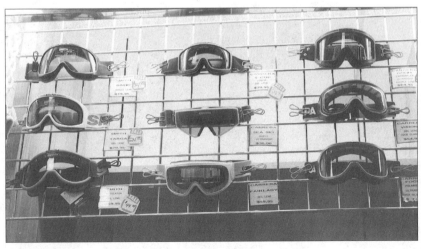

Herb Gordon

Point the tips backwards when you lock your skis onto a ski rack. Bindings should be covered to protect them from salt spray on winter highways.

2. Sun block. Use only one with an SPF factor of 25 for young and sensitive skin at high altitudes. Apply per directions.

2a. Sunburn ointment.

3. A boot bag. Every member of the family should have his or her own. The bag, usually with an outside zipper pocket, is designed to hold one pair of boots. Add a small bag that can slide into the bag with the boots. Add a small bag that can slide into the bag with the boots. The small bag should be large enough to hold your cap, neck gaiter or face mask, ski gloves, and goggles.

Our family policy is that, as soon as we walk into the front door after a ski trip, each of us is responsible for assuring that all his or her equipment is cleaned, dried, and repacked before the bag—fully ready for the next assault on the slopes—is put away.

3a. The side pocket. I carry a small pair of pliers, one small regular and one Phillips-head screwdriver, a tube of fluorocarbon ski wax, a hand-held edge sharpener, a cable ski lock, a couple extra bags of the hand- and foot-warmer chemicals sold at every ski shop today, a pack of safety pins, a tiny hand-winding table alarm clock (the battery never runs down), a small waterproof flashlight (always stocked with fresh batteries before a trip), a candle and matches sealed in a plastic pouch, two self-stick wall hooks (to slap onto that condo bathroom or closet door that has no wall hangers for guests), and assorted undeterminables. Someday I've got to clean out that pocket.

4. A ski bag. Ski bags come in several styles. There are the tough fabric bags that completely enclose one or two sets of skis. There are full-length plastic tubes for one or two pairs of skis. And there are half-sized fabric bags that cover only the ski bindings, to protect them when the skis are mounted on a car. Better fabric bags, both for bindings and for complete skis, are lined with padding.

5. Car racks. It's fairly standard for a set of car racks to carry four pairs of skis. If your rack doesn't lock in the skis, follow the old adage: Man, don't let 'em out of your sight.

6. Combination boot and traveling bag. This has space at each end for a boot, while the large interior can be filled with clothing. It's great for the ski traveler but usually too large for overhead storage on the plane; it'll have to be checked through.

7. Battery-operated boot heaters. With special wiring feeding current from rechargeable batteries to electronic heating elements in the toe area of the insole, these will keep your feet toasty even in the arctic chill of a three-dog night. Pay heed: Check the price before you have them installed in your boots.

8. Headband. For those days when it's too warm to wear a cap and your long hair must be controlled.

9. Fanny pack—waterproof. This is better than pockets for carrying everything from a trail map, lunch money, and a tube of lip salve to a sandwich.

10. Extra camera batteries. The colder it is, the more quickly older batteries drop dead. Protect a camera by carrying it inside your ski jacket or fanny pack with—but of course—an extra roll of film for that moment when you run out on the mountain.

11. Après-ski boots. As elaborate as you want and can afford.

5

We're All Skiers

The ski industry has suddenly begun to realize that 40 percent of the skiers on any mountain are women—and women have special needs, from boots designed specifically for their feet to lessons in basic and advanced ski techniques. Seniors, too, can start to ski or improve their skiing through ski organizations, as well as through ski resorts—which are now adding instructional and special programs for senior skiers. And miracle skiers are those with physical problems or handicaps who, with help from special organizations and programs at many ski resorts, are also skiing those wonderful winter slopes.

WOMEN ON SKIS

Yes, women do ski differently than men. Which, of course, has no bearing whatsoever upon their ability to ski. Women race. Women ski the extreme. Women range from klutzes to superb experts. Even as men do.

But because of their slightly different physical structure, they also ski a bit differently than men do. The differences are small—but important.

Men have a narrow pelvis and legs that sort of bow out at the knees. Women usually have a wider pelvis, a lower center of gravity, and knees that bow slightly in.

As novices, women have a penchant for skiing for skiing with their backsides sticking farther out than a man's, and to ski knock-kneed. This has nothing to do with their ability to learn—only with their physical shape.

Does this suggest that women should be taught differently than men? The clear-cut answer is actually a slightly foggy "yes and no." Translation: Instructors must be fully cognizant of the fact that—because of physical differences, not any lack of ability—women actually appear different when skiing, especially in the early learning stages.

Instructors, says one ski authority of Sun Valley's special programs for women, must also be sensitive to the emotional differences between men and women. This can be significant if, for instance, in a mixed-gender class an instructor unwittingly praises men who seem to acquire the "appropriate" skills faster than women.

However, women usually learn to snowplow more quickly than their male companions because the snowplow stance is more natural to their physical shape. With his bow legs, a man may find a wide stance uncomfortable and compensate by increasing the pressure on the inside edges of his skis. But his female companion finds it easier to push her tails apart and roll her knees inward.

Even among experienced skiers, men and women still differ slightly in their techniques. It's easier for a man to keep his skis close together when racing down the fall line than it is for a woman. On a traverse, a woman will angle her body farther from the slope than a man, simply because of her lower center of gravity. In a parallel turn, if a woman wants to ski in a closed stance, she may find it necessary to press one knee against the other; a man's slightly bowed knees enable him to keep his feet close together without such pressure.

Even as we age, men's and women's physical shapes change differently. Older men tend to develop a paunch; older women, larger thighs. Ski experts stress how important it is for instructors working with senior skiers to recognize that these physical changes influence the way older men and women ski.

Women's Programs

The ski resort industry has come only within the past few years to recognize what every coach, regardless of the sport, has known for generations: Women and men differ in body and muscle structure and often in temperament; these differences affect the way each learns and becomes proficient.

Although most resorts group men and women into the same never-ever classes, a few now offer beginner classes exclusively for women and taught by women. In addition, a steadily increasing number hold a broad range of special clinics and activities for women, and by women, throughout the winter.

Olympic gold- and silver-medalist Diann Roffe-Steinrotter, a spokeswoman for National Women's Ski Week, says there's no dispute that almost every woman, from beginner to mountain expert, will learn something of special benefit to her in a women's program with women teachers.

Claudia Carbone, author of *Women Ski*, believes that "too many women have been frustrated while trying to ski. Everyone in the ski industry can and should help women enjoy snow activities more."

On a snow holiday in the dramatic mountains of the Whistler/Blackcomb resort in western British Columbia, I spent one day in a women-only three-day program, skiing with a group of six women, all good intermediate skiers in their 30s and 40s, and their dynamic female instructor. Eye-opening.

Laughing, learning, moving from high intermediate to black-diamond trails, they were all obviously keen to improve. Their instructor was cheerful and enthusiastic, filled with words of praise, pushing them to a level none had reached in their past years of playing on snowy runs and avoiding steep moguls. Never suggesting anyone was "doing it better" than anyone else. They tackled moguls. Not with a fearless need to blast through, but with a quieter skill.

As they skied, their instructor occasionally paused to watch each soar past, then stopped her to offer a few hints about her ski posture. If it seemed to my unskilled eye that some had more backside sticking out, this was not a problem to the instructor. "They're built like women," she told me. "They ski with a woman's posture." Pause. "Not a man's."

When the last trail was skied and the women crowded noisily into the base lodge for a "farewell picnic," I asked what had been the most interesting aspect of the program.

Unanimously, they agreed on one special point: They had never been intimidated. Not by a male instructor trying to prove his own prowess or urging them to adopt a ski posture better suited to a man's structure; not by men in the group pushing to outperfrom everyone.

"The best learning experience I've ever had on skis" was how one woman expressed it. "Just great."

Herb Gordon

A female instructor with six women students at a three-day ski program for women, Whistler, British Columbia.

Here are some examples of the special women's programs increasingly offered by ski resorts across the nation:

Kirkwood, one of the cluster of ski areas in Lake Tahoe, has a series of both one- and three-day clinics that are tailored to the skill level of the participants and that are run by women, utilizing women-centered instruction. It also offers one three-day clinic for intermediate and advanced skiers that includes discussions on "How to Avoid Injury" and "Fitness for Skiing."

At Heavenly Valley, three-day seminars are taught by female instructors to help women skiers "improve their skills in a relaxed atmosphere."

Loon Mountain, in New Hampshire, holds three-day "Women's Getaways" created, organized, and taught by women. Its goal: "To elevate your level of skiing and to overcome fears of difficult terrain and conditions through group enthusiasm, determination and support."

Vail, in Colorado's Rockies, has both three- and five-day programs "for women who feel they've reached a plateau in their skiing and want a breakthrough." The women-only programs also include après-ski workshops; one focuses on "equipment as it applies to women" and another, led by a sports psychologist, addresses "fear and how to deal with it."

In addition to its long-established Women's Ski Escape programs, Killington has instituted a daily Women's Mountain School. One Killington executive says the mountain classes were inaugurated "as an effort to introduce more teaching programs designed specifically to educate women how to use their unique physical characteristics to reach their peak skiing potential." The two-hour programs are taught by female instructors.

Mammoth Mountain in California, Stowe in Vermont, and Winter Park in Colorado cooperate in a series of women's ski programs for National Women's Ski Week in mid-January. Each area offers a variety of self-help seminars, on-hill clinics, and demonstrations of skis, boots, and bindings.

Not all ski areas offer instruction or seminars for women. For the woman interested in any level of women-oriented program, from simply learning how to ski to skiing the extreme, I advise inquiring into the programs offered at a resort before booking a ski holiday.

Equipment and Clothing

Along with the swiftly spreading interest in distinctive training programs for women, there's a growing trend among manufacturers to design gear and equipment specifically for female skiers. For example:

Boots

For years it was customary in the boot industry to mark smaller models "F" and larger models "M." However, many companies now make boots shaped particularly for women, who have a narrower ankle, longer toes, a higher instep and arch, and longer calves, which extend farther into boots than a man's. Hint for a woman shopping for new boots: If they're too tight around your calf it's probably because the particular manufacturer is still packaging a smaller-sized man's boot with a softer inner lining, coloring the snaps pink, and calling it a woman's model, rather than offering a design specifically for a woman's foot.

The key to a good fit is to find the one closest to your own foot. Try at least three different makes of boots when purchasing, regardless of whether the box they come in is labeled male or female. The lable does not ensure comfort. A proper fit does.

One boot-buying technique recommended by the experts at *Snow Country* magazine is to sample different and smaller sizes, regardless of what the boot salesclerk measured you for. "Make sure," says *Snow Country*, "the salesperson pulls out the inner boot and fits the empty shell to your foot. This practice provides the most accurate sizing. Even if one size boot seems to fit properly, try the next size down to be sure you've found the smallest shell that fits comfortably."

Try on boots only with the same socks and, if possible, underwear and in-the-boot ski pants that you wear when skiing. The ski shop has a dressing room.

Since many women have difficulty putting forward pressure on their ski tips because they carry more of their weight in their thighs and backsides, it will help to buy a boot with a soft forward flex. Heel lifts, as well as orthotic inserts, can also be used to increase the pressure on the boot tips.

More expensive, but more effective, is to have the boot customized and performance-tuned by a skilled technician. This often means manipulating such things as the foot and the heel height, or adjusting the forward lean and cuff alignment, or even mounting the bindings 1 to 3 cm forward of the mark, to increase pressure on the tips.

Skis

How interested are ski manufacturers in producing skis in all price ranges that are suited for women? The answer for years was: "Well, golly, we've always made skis for the lighter male that are great for women, too."

However, there are now, finally, skis specifically designed for women—especially in the higher price ranges—whose abilities range from intermediate to racer. Compared to unisex skis these are only slightly different in shape, but they're softer both longitudinally and torsionally. However, unisex models are still the basic offering for the beginner and low intermediate skier in the lower price ranges.

New hourglass skis are basically unisex.

The annual buyers'-guide issues of major ski magazines report on the best women's skis as selected by their own female testers.

Bindings

There's no argument: A binding is a binding. But there is increasing skepticism over what some consider the failure of manufacturers to put enough research or effort into determining whether bindings should be adapted especially for women, rather than produced in unisex patterns. Many women need to have a mounting moved slightly forward of the position marked on the ski, and this raises the questions of whether bindings, or skis, should offer alternative setting points for women, and whether bindings would be more effective if designed for women.

Poles

Gloves are made with slightly different designs for men and for women. Poles that are held in gloved hands are neither designated nor made differently for men and women. Should pole grips, like gloves, be made to different specifications for each sex?

Clothing

Finally, there's the question whether designers of the active woman's outdoor and ski wardrobe could fashion ski pants better suited for female needs—perhaps by tailoring them with a zippered drop seat.

SKIING SENIORS

A half-dozen women skiers lining up to race down a long, steep pitch ribbed each other mercilessly.

"Oh, you haven't got a chance. Why, you're too old to go racing."

"Old? You've got me beat by ten years."

"Right. I've got you beat. But it's gonna be on this run, not on the calendar."

"My old man says it's time to stop racing."

"And what does his 'old lady' say to that?"

At the gate the starter, a young and cheerful man obviously enjoying his role, called out for the women in the race to line up. "Show them what you can do, baby," he winked at the first racer.

"This baby has been showing them what she could do for fifty years," she called back, bending forward, her face suddenly intent on only one goal: to win the women's-division races of the 70+ Ski Club's annual March convention at Hunter Mountain in the Catskills.

The women had one thing in common: As members of 70+ they all were 70 or older. And, like the men in the club races, they were challenging each other on Racer's Edge, a course long and steep enough for international professional racers.

It's an exhilarating experience simply watching senior skiers compete in timed races on snowy pitches too difficult for most of the recreational skiers who throng the slopes of Hunter Mountain.

The 70+ Ski Club was organized by Lloyd Lambert—who first donned wooden skis as a kid playing on the snows of the Adirondacks about the time of World War I—in 1977. By 1955 more than 14,000 member worldwide were wearing its distinctive red-and-white shoulder patch. Its annual convention is held at Hunter Mountain.

These 70+ skiers, as well as the thousands of members of a cluster of other ski clubs for seniors who ardently, or gently, challenge the slopes in winter, are visible proof that skiing is a sport without age barriers. It's estimated that a quarter-million skiers in the mid-1990s were 55 or older. Within the next 10 years, the United Ski Industries Association expects that number to grow by at least another 100,000.

You don't need to be a lifelong skier who's crossed the threshold into maturity to join any of these ski organizations. Age is the only criterion. No previous experience necessary.

Health Considerations and Benefits

Dr. Wade Johnson, a New York internist whose patients are primarily seniors, says there's only one compelling factor for the 50-and-older man or woman to consider when taking up any physical sports, including skiing, for the first time: good health! A thorough physical examination is imperative for first-timers of advancing years before they put on skis—"just as it is for seniors who want to start exercising or take up any active sport."

Dr. Johnson has this word of caution, though, for the over-50 who hasn't been especially physically active: "Begin working out gradually to improve the cardiovascular system, along with the muscles. Regular warm-up exercises that involve bending and twisting are a real asset."

He says that since cross-country skiing is more demanding on the body than downhill, "the cross-country addict has got to be in better physical condition, especially where the cardiovascular system is concerned, than the easygoing downhiller.

"When you're skiing at a resort you ride uphill and ski down. There certainly are no lifts when you're pushing yourself along a cross-country trail through the woods."

Dr. Johnson sounds one very practical note of warning for senior skiers. "It doesn't make any difference if you're skiing a big resort, or a backcountry trail—always ski with a companion. If something goes wrong, your chances of avoiding a rough problem are a lot better if you have a buddy alongside to help out."

He agrees with a point often made—with considerable enthusiasm—by senior skiers: Skiers can enjoy relaxed alpine skiing on easy runs or push themselves as far as they want to. The choice is totally theirs.

The good doctor has several last words for seniors: "Skiing? It does wonders for you. Go. Go."

Researchers have long documented improvements in the health and well-being of seniors who are physically active. They've found that, to enjoy the benefits, it's never too late to start.

Here are some of the benefits energetic seniors enjoy, according to the President's Council on Physical Fitness:

Heart disease and stroke: Exercise helps reduce the risk of these by lowering blood pressure, raising the level of beneficial cholesterol, and reducing the risk of blood clots.

Cancer: Exercise lowers the risk of colon cancer.

Depression: Any sport that requires physical skill has long been recognized as helping seniors overcome clinical depression. This is especially true of those sports that are noncompetitive, where there's no "loser" and no "winner." Skiing is cited by Dr. Johnson as "amazingly effective" in preventing depression.

Memory: Skiing fosters clearer thinking and faster reaction time, as does any active sport or regular exercise. Dr. Johnson says that even brief periods of skiing can result in immediate memory improvement in older adults.

Osteoporosis: At any age exercise and physical activity increase the density of bones and reduce the risk of fracture. It's not the exuberant 70-

70+ Ski Club members at an annual meeting, Hunter Mountain.

year-old woman skiing down the slopes of Grand Targhee who'll break her leg in a fall. It's more apt to be her lethargic sister, falling when she gets up to change movies on the VCR.

Diabetes: Those physically active are less likely to develop it after 50.

Immunity: Exercise at any age aids the circulation of the immune cells that fight infections. The physically energetic catch fewer colds. It's their friends sitting in stuffy offices while the wind and snow blow outside who have the stuffy noses or the flu.

Arthritis: Over 65 this is common to almost everyone. Both general and stretching exercises and physical activities can reduce pain.

Sleep: It doesn't take a corps of researchers to knows that after a good day on the mountains, the weary senior falls asleep more quickly and enjoys better-quality sleep than his sedentary friend hunched in a chair watching television.

Love: Whether it's because skiing raises the testosterone level in men, or because the wind in their hair stirs romantic thoughts in women, senior skiers are as renowned as their younger mountain counterparts for their passionate desire for passion. C'est la vie!

For the Eager Seniors

A steadily increasing number of ski resorts in every region of the nation have set up learn-to-ski programs for older persons who have a long-buried, or suddenly born, desire to join their grandchildren on the slopes. Instructors are inevitably themselves seniors.

Almost every ski area in the United States also offers seniors discounts on lift tickets. Many offer free skiing to members of the 70+ Ski Club. Free or heavily discounted lift tickets for seniors are customary throughout Europe. In addition, special discount packages are widely available to seniors. The following are examples of the programs generally available at major destination resorts:

Sun Valley, Idaho. Prime Time Special discount packages in January and early February for skiers 60 and over include a welcome reception and a special evening dinner with dancing, plus a lift ticket for five out of six days, lessons, mountain tours, and a senior race. For information: (800) 786-8259.

Purgatory, Colorado. The SnoMasters Classic programs for skiers 55 and older include a reduced-rate lift ticket and discounts on rentals, lodging, food, and lessons. For information: (303) 247-9000.

Waterville Valley, New Hampshire. The Silver Streak program involves a host of discounted activities, as well as discounted lift tickets. For information: (603) 236-8311.

Aspen, Colorado. Fit Over Fifty offers seminars on subjects from nutrition to finance, and a five-day program that includes lodging, lessons, and lift tickets. For information: (800) 952-1616.

Park City, Utah. It's Never Too Late, for those 50 and older, includes learn-to-ski programs, and mountain classes for experienced skiers. All instructors are seniors. For information: (801) 649-8111.

Stratton, Vermont. Club 62, for skiers 62 and older, offers lessons and mountain tours twice weekly. For information: (802) 297-2200.

Badger Pass, Yosemite National Park. Silver Skier, for those 60 and older, includes a free season pass and beginner lessons. For information: (209) 372-1330.

Because of the steady increase in the number of ski areas that run special programs or offer discount packages for seniors, ask your favorite ski resort what its policies and programs are. If it doesn't offer seniors a discount, hey, go elsewhere.

Senior Skiier Network
In 1996, the Professional Ski Instructors of America, Eastern Education Foundation, developed a program that provides: 1) continuous skill development for seniors; 2) opportunities for seniors to explore new challenges in a safe environment; and 3) opportunities for seniors to share ski activities with peers.

Modeled after the Senior Skier Development Program at the Ski Windham resort, Windham, New York, the Senior Skier Network is composed of some 50 ski areas throughout the East that offer midweek senior programs, including lessons and supervised skiing sessions led by a PSI peer instructor. The programs are open to skiers of all levels, including never-evers.

Ski Clubs
The following are some of the senior ski clubs throughout the nation:

70+ Ski Club. Lifetime membership for $5 plus proof of age. Members receive a list of ski resorts throughout the world that offer free skiing, or major discounts, to members; the club sponsors ski trips to other countries. For information: Lloyd Lambert, 104 East Side Drive, Ballston Lake, NY 12019.

Over the Hill Gang. For skiers 50 and older, with chapters throughout the country. In addition to skiing, the group sponsors other outdoor activities for members. For information: Over the Hill Gang, 13791 East Rice Place, Suite 101, Aurora, CO 80015.

Elderhostel. Learn-to-ski classes are held at the Sunday River ski resort in Maine. The skiing is part of academic programs. For information: Elderhostel in Boston, (617) 426-8056.

Ski Meisters. A Denver-based group for skiers 50 and older. Members ski chiefly at Winter Park, Colorado, in guided groups. For information: Ski Meisters, Box 36338, Denver, CO 80236.

Skiing Grandmothers. Always recognizable by their cheerful red ski suits with blue cowboy hats, members are involved in ski-related charities and travel. Most are from the Southwest and Colorado, but the club is open to all grandmother skiers. For information: La Nelle Townley, 10027 Cedar Creek, Houston, TX 77042.

Over Eighty Ski Club. For those 80 and older. Members have their names listed on a Scroll of Distinction at the U.S. Ski Hall of Fame. Membership requires a $25 donation to the hall of fame. For information: Ray Leverton, Box 191, Ishpeming, MI 49849-0191.

Physical Fitness Guides

Several excellent guides are available for seniors who want to improve their physical condition. They include:

A 32-page illustrated manual, " 'Pep Up Your Life': A Fitness Book for Mid-Life and Older Persons," was prepared under the guidance of the President's Council on Physical Fitness and Sports and the American Association of Retired Persons. Free copies are available from the American Association of Retired Persons, Fulfillment Department, 601 E Street N.W., Washington, DC 20036.

The National Association for Human Development has three booklets on exercises—basic, moderate, and advanced—for people 60 and older. Each costs $3 and can be purchased from the association at 1424 16th Street N.W., Washington, DC 20036.

"Senior Shape-Up," which includes two audiotapes and a 41-page manual, is available for $36 from Yablon Enterprises, Inc., P.O. Box 7475, Steelton, PA 17113. Yablon produced the material in cooperation with Creative Fitness, Inc.

MIRACLE SKIERS

It wasn't precisely the ideal day for skiing. The wind was gusting up to 20 miles an hour, kicking up showers of powder snow and laying bare the icy crud underneath. Low clouds scudded across the sky.

It was, on the other hand, a day to go into the base lodge early for a long lunch and watch bewhiskered men rub the icicles from their beards as they walked through the swinging doors into the crowded, steamy building.

After only a couple hours fighting the elements, my wife and I decided it was time to get out of the weather and into, as W. C. Fields once said, a dry martini, when for the first time I saw a disabled person on skis.

He was a younger man, probably in his mid-20s, with one leg amputated below the knee, skiing on his good leg while keeping his balance with poles that had small skis—instead of baskets—on the bottoms.

A few moments later, as we swooshed down a steep shortcut to the base lodge, the one-legged skier was right behind us. At the bottom of the pitch we all stopped briefly. He grinned. "Quite a day," he said.

"We've about had it for this morning," I said. "You going in to warm up?"

"Oh, hell no," he laughed. "I get warm skiing."

He waved to us, turned, and pushed himself toward a nearby chairlift.

We were awed watching this one-legged man skiing, smiling, reveling in the pursuit of the same challenge and adventure as those of us without any physical handicaps.

He stood patiently in the lift line, though several skiers tried to edge aside so he could crowd ahead. No way. He was a skier. No more. No less. Asking nothing that any able-bodied skier wouldn't.

A one-legged skier challenges the slopes.

The chairlift seated two skiers, side by side. He and another skier slid in front of an empty chair as it swung around the anchor pylon, and dropped into the seat. No fuss. He was on his way up. The wind grew a bit stronger.

My wife said, "How can he stand this weather?"

I said, "We ski in it. He does, too."

I was filled with admiration for this ordinary miracle of life on the snow. A one-legged man skiing.

Not Unusual Today

Today, the sight of the physically impaired is increasingly common on the ski runs of America. People of all ages, from kids to seniors, are on the slopes, enjoying the thrill of skiing, without letting their physical or mental disabilities keep them off the mountains.

Scott Ingram, director of the Breckenridge Outdoor Education Center, Colorado, one of several distinguished institutions in the nation that teaches the disabled to enjoy the out-of-doors doing everything from skiing and canoeing to backpacking, says these activities help the handicapped escape from what was once an isolated way of life.

"The learn self-confidence and self-esteem. They find a new level of independence in themselves," he says.

People with special needs are taught how to ski at the Breckenridge center. Lessons are offered both to individuals and groups throughout the ski season. Some 1,000 participants each year come from rehabilitation centers, individual living centers for the disabled, and hospitals.

Ingram says many of the disabled have been grossly overprotected by parents, siblings, schools, and society. "Some have never been permitted to climb on the back of a couch, much less climb onto a chairlift."

Once exposed to the world of skiing—under the careful guidance of trained volunteers—participants begin to place their trust in others. Ingram says he still finds it one of the most meaningful activities of his own life to watch them discover that "they are not that unusual, after all, and that they can do anything—if they put their minds to it."

Hal O'Leary, founder and director of the National Sports Center for the Disabled, at Winter Park, Colorado, says of the physically challenged: "If there is a limitation in what they can do, it is not a failure.

A skier with paralyzed legs "skis" sitting on a mono-sled, controlled by two small hand-skis.

It is only temporary—until adaptive equipment is designed and methods discovered that permit success."

With a full-time staff of 13, and 850 volunteers, Winter Park gives more than 14,000 lessons a year to 2,500 skiers with 45 types of disabilities. A sign above its center reads: IN CELEBRATION OF THE HUMAN SPIRIT.

Techniques Differ

Impaired skiers must maneuver and traverse and slalom, just as the non-handicapped. The techniques and equipment used, however, do differ.

The two principal systems for skiers with physical problems are those for skiers who can ski while standing and those for the disabled who can ski only while sitting. Standees include those with a single lower extremity, skiers who've lost one or both upper extremities, and blind and low-vision skiers. Sit-skiers are those who've lost both legs, paraplegics, quadriplegics, and skiers with other physical problems.

Standing skiers use a one-, three-, or four-track technique, depending on the number of tracks left in the snow.

One-trackers are the most skillful. They need no special equipment—just one ski and a pair of regular poles. In 1987–88, Diana Golden was named Ski Racing's U.S. Alpine Skier of the Year. She's a one-track skier, and a seven-time world champion.

The lone skier we saw whipping down the slopes with all the skill of my wife or myself was a three-track skier. He was skiing on one leg and using two outriggers—forearm crutch-style ski poles with short skis attached to them. The outriggers give added balance and steering ability.

Four-trackers are those who can ski on two skis but need the stabilization of outriggers.

Skiers unable to stand are sit-skiers. They use one of two types of equipment: a sled, or a seat mounted on a mono-ski.

The sled-skier flies down the mountains in a Norwegian *pulk*—a sled shaped much like a child's pedal car—or a molded sled. He uses two short ski poles to reach over the sides of the sled for guidance, and to push himself along.

The seat-skier uses a seat mounted on a *mono-ski*—a ski that's almost as wide as a snowboard but as long as a regular ski. The seat is much higher than that in a pulk.

Like the sled-skier, the seat-skier has two short ski poles, which may be either outrigger style or regular, for balance or for pushing herself along when the slope flattens out.

With the exceptions of the blind and sled-skiers, the physically handicapped can often ride the chairlifts by themselves. Sled-skiers need special, caring assistants to load them and their sleds onto the lifts.

Disabled Competitions

Ski competitions for both standing and sitting skiers are held throughout the country and in Europe. Both Aspen Highlands and Mount Hood Meadows ski resorts have hosted the U.S. championships. The 1990 World Disabled Championships were held at Winter Park, Colorado; the 1992 championships were held at Breckenridge, Colorado.

An increasing number of ski areas, eastern and western, offer ski programs for persons with disabilities and make their resort facilities accessible to them. Among the permanent, on-mountain ski schools are:

Breckenridge Outdoor Education Center, Box 697, Breckenridge, CO 80424; (303) 453-6422.

National Sports Center for the Disabled, Box 36, Winter Park, CO 80482; (303) 726-5514.

Tahoe Handicapped Ski School at Alpine Meadows. Offices: 5926 Illinois Avenue, Orangevale, CA 95662; (916) 989-0402.

Bear Mountain, P.O. Box 6812, Big Bear Lake, CA; (714) 585-2519. Bear Mountain is about three hours east of Los Angeles.

Ski Windham, 1A Lincoln Avenue, Albany, NY 12205; (518) 452-6095. Ski Windham is about two-and-a-half hours north of New York City.

Park City Handicapped Sports Association, Box 680286, Park City, UT 84068; (801) 649-3991.

New England Handicapped Sportsmen's Association, with ski facilities at Haystack Mountain, Vermont. Offices: 26 McFarlin Road, Chelmsford, MA 01824; (508) 256-3240.

Aspen Handicapped Skiers Association, c/o Edwin Lucks, P.O. Box 5429, Snowmass Village, CO 81615.

Durango/Purgatory Handicapped Sports Association, P.O. Box 1884, Durango, CO 81302.

Horizons, c/o Christine K. Collins, P.O. Box 774867, Steamboat Springs, CO 80477.

Waterville Valley Ski Touring Center, Town Square, Waterville, NH 03215.

There are a number of associations in the United States and Canada whose goals are to bring those with special physical problems into the world of sports.

The largest in the United States is the National Handicapped Sports and Recreation Association. The association has 86 local chapters and affiliates. The NHS holds learn-to-ski clinics throughout the country and sponsors the annual Ski Spectacular for Disabled Skiers in Breckenridge. For information write the association at 451 Hungerford Drive, Suite 100, Rockville, MD 20850; (301) 217-0960.

The Canadian Association for Disabled Skiing is the national association for eight divisions of disabled skiing organizations in Canada. For information write: Box 307, Kimberly, British Columbia, VIA 2Y9, CANADA; (604) 427-7712.

6

Kids

Y ou start them off knowing only too well—but not accepting it—
the possibility that one day they'll outski you. There's a while to go
before they do, though—and here are some fine hints on what every
parent needs to know, beginning with the welcome even *diapered* infants
now get at ski resorts. There are age-level guidelines—not cast in stone,
but useful—for youngsters still in play school, and for beginners in the
four-to-six set, as well as for sevens and older. Look at the benefits of ski
schools; understand how you can help your eager offspring become spir-
ited yet controlled skiers; heed the advice about saving money when
buying or renting equipment. And kids gotta keep warm, too, so here are
some suggestions for ensuring that they're comfortable on the slopes.

SKIING KIDS

Wedge your kid's feet into ski boots, lock them onto a pair of skis, and,
sooner or sometime in the near future, a hoary joke will become a reality.

Here's how it happened in the Gordon family: We were on a ski holiday, enjoying the snow-clad, soaring mountains at Colorado's Steamboat
Springs. A powerful, short storm swept across the area one day, dumping
more than a foot of powdery snow. The next morning we were up early,
hustling to catch the first lifts, dazzled by the thought of hitting snow that
the plows were quickly packing down on all but the black and double-
black pitches.

Splendid. We were as delirious as the several thousand other skiers
around us when the sun burst through the clouds in midmorning.

Skiing was almost nonstop. At the bottom of every run the girls, then 12 years old, were the first ones onto the next chair up. I must admit to a sense of inner excitement watching them, their golden red hair flying in the wind, as they carved their way down the packed-powder runs and bounced through the bumps with élan and skill.

Coasting to a stop at the base area after a long, exhausting run, my wife said she was ready for lunch. I sighed that my weary bones, too, were groaning for a rest.

"It's too early, Mom," the girls complained. "Can't we take one more run first?"

My wife turned to me. "You want to go with them? I've got to head for the john. I'll meet you all in the cafeteria."

"Okay, Dad," they shouted. "Let's go." I followed, reluctantly.

Climbing out of the gondola that had carried us swiftly to the summit, the girls headed immediately toward black and double-black pitches covered with powder snow untouched by the cats.

"We haven't gone down this way," one called out. "This is the way," the other yelled at me.

I hesitated. I'd skied those steeps in the past but now, well, I stopped and looked down.

It was then I heard the saddest words on the mountain: "Follow us, Dad."

I smiled, wan and weary, and said: "Hey, go on. I'll meet you at the bottom." Their words, as they flashed over the crest and hurtled down, kept rattling around in my ears: "Follow us, Dad."

I caught up with them at the cafeteria, jammed with hungry skiers. They already had their platters heaped with food and were waiting at a table with their mom by the time I'd locked up my skis and wobbled inside.

Yes, it happens. Young legs. Bodies alive with vibrant muscle. Anxious to challenge whatever the mountains offer. And the skill to succeed.

"Follow us, Dad."

Sooner or later, every skiing parent will hear those words.

Before it happens to you, let's look at some of the key ingredients in taking kids, from three-month-olds to teenagers, skiing.

Infants

One of the blessings today for new parents who ski is that almost all resorts, from the small gems to the crown jewels, have excellent facilities to baby-sit infants as young as three months. Quite an improvement over what we encountered when we wanted to take our infant twins skiing in the late 1970s.

At that time in all New England only three ski areas accepted children as young as two, and then only if they were toilet trained. The usual minimum age to put children in a day-care center was three. As they'd been doing since skiing become a nationwide sport after World War II, most ski areas simply smiled at parents foolish enough to want to put their babies into a nursery right there on the mountain. They would, however, recommend local baby-sitters to care for the wee wee set while Mom and Dad were on the slopes.

Changing times.

Not only are nurseries integral to most ski areas today, but the resorts compete with each other in the quality of their facilities. A word of caution is necessary, though, for parents taking their gurgling diaper-clad offspring to a ski area for the first time: Call before you make your travel plans. Question its infant and nursery programs, even if you're bound for a resort you knew well in the years before you became parents.

Be specific: Is the nursery separate from the play area for older children? What's the minimum age? In some areas, it's as young as six weeks. While most states require that nursery attendants be qualified and licensed, some don't. As about the attendants' personal qualifications.

A few smaller resorts still require parents to take out their babies during the lunch hour. This can be a problem, naturally, if you're far from the nursery when the local fire department toots its noon whistle.

Two- and Three-Year-Olds

Once your children are old enough to be out of cribs, ski resorts generally offer excellent day-care facilities, including well-equipped indoor play areas with toys, games, slides, and swings, and staffs trained in working with children.

The more progressive ski day-care centers teach some skills to children once they reach the age of three. These skills may range from sliding around on skis inside the recreation room to a couple hours a day on the snowy slopes outside the children's center, learning how to snowplow, the snowplow turn, and easy gliding on the snow.

There are exceptions, of course, but most children don't have the coordination and muscle control to learn to ski until about the age of four, regardless of the fact that too many parents believe their children are going to be Olympic champs in a couple years. Parents with children in this almost-the-right-age bracket can play games involving skiing, but beware: Do not push your youngsters beyond their level of comfort and fun. That can be a turn-off, not a turn-on.

Kiddie Games

Here are some of the games we played on the slopes with Hilary and Rebecca before they actually took lessons. Their first ski boots were their own little hiking boots, and their skis were cheap plastic tie-ons:

Pull and catch: We helped the children get to the top of a small, easy slope. While Gail stood at the stop and pointed first one, then the other, downhill, I waited at the bottom to catch them as they coasted by.

Between the legs: This was far more complicated. The basic requirement was a gentle run that neither taxed our own ski skills nor made the children nervous. We found the Snowshed area at Killington, a ¾-mile-long slope as smooth as a tilted billiard table, ideal. Gail and I each took one child and rode the slow-moving chairlift to the top. Then we skied leisurely down, each holding a girl between our legs. With giggles of joy, the girls would try to "get down first," challenging Mom or Dad to go faster, faster.

As the youngsters gained in confidence, we began letting them ski by themselves—almost. Instead of wedging them between our legs, we looped a piece of rope around them and, while holding it, let them ski a couple feet in front of us.

On occasion there were falls. Nothing that brushing off the snow wouldn't cure. Minor accidents never curbed the girls' exuberant feeling about skiing.

Follow me: While each girl held onto a ski pole, we pulled her quickly across the flat snows near the base lodge.

Making circles: In this game we encouraged the children to "ski in circles on their skis," an introduction to maneuvering.

Four- to Six-Year-Olds

This age level is time for the real world and real skis and a real decision for the majority of young ones. A decision by parents to have their child

First, let Dad straighten out your skis. Now . . .

learn to ski, even at this age, must be based on an important fact: The child must actually want to learn. One thing all ski experts agree on is the need to be patient and not push a child who, for whatever reason, is reluctant to ski now, but may tomorrow.

In other words, a child is ready to ski when he wants to ski. Not when parents feel he is.

Every parent must then make a second decision: Are you going to teach your child, or will you put him into ski school?

Before answering that question, meditate upon the words of an old skiing friend of mine, the late I. William Berry, a lifelong skiing addict, ski writer, one-time executive editor of *Ski* magazine, past president of the Eastern Ski Writers Association, and father of two children who are dynamite on the slopes, about who should teach children the skills of skiing: "Put them in [ski] school, unless you happen to be a certified instructor— at which time you already know enough to put them in [ski] school without my saying so."

Go for it.

Seven and Older

By the time your children reach the age of seven, the quality of their instructors is far more important than the size of the learning area or the indoor facilities. Now the kids meet with the ski school instructors at a designated outside area—almost always separate from where adults taking lessons meet.

Groupings are based on two factors: age and ability. The 7s-to-10s or -12s are separated from the teenagers. But naturally. Would your teenager even consider being in a ski class with a seven-year-old? Within the age groups, children are broken into classes based upon skiing skills. Never-evers are always in a class by themselves.

The normal ratio of instructors to students in the older age groups is 1:6 for the never-evers, and perhaps 1:8 for others. Never waste money putting a young learner in a class of more than eight skiers, whether the ski school lasts for a week or a weekend.

In the seven-and-older bracket, the usual routine calls for a couple hours of ski lessons in the morning; a cheerful, noisy lunch with the instructor, generally in a reserved section of a base lodge or on-mountain restaurant; and an afternoon of more lessons.

SKI SCHOOL OR SKI LESSONS?

It's less effective for a child to learn skiing by taking an occasional lesson on a busy weekend than by spending a week in a ski school. Even eager adults can pick up only a smidgen of skiing techniques in an hour-and-a-half lesson with a harried instructor trying to give 10, or even more, rank beginners an idea of the skills required to cruise down a high mountain on powder snow.

Whatever a child learns taking weekend lessons—while remarkably helpful—can also be half forgotten in the dry spell until the family heads again for the slopes and another lesson or two.

The situation is quite different, however, when it comes to a one-week stay in a ski school.

For five days there are lessons every morning and every afternoon. The same instructor stays with the same ebullient youngsters for the entire week. He or she is quick to spot the child that needs special help. The skills the new skiers learn in the morning are rehearsed in the afternoon.

The progress from this day-after-day series of lessons is remarkable. Never-evers are, by the end of the week, following an instructor skiing down an easy blue mountain run. Those who pick up skills quickly may even be chasing after a fast-moving instructor leading them down the challenge of the advanced blue trails.

If you choose the ski school route, familiarize yourself with the school of your choice before hauling out the credit cards to pay for putting your youngster in one: Is there a well-equipped play area where the younger children, the five- to seven-year-olds, can rest when they're not out ski-ing, with its own kitchen, lunch room, and bathrooms, or do the kids need to tromp through the bewildering noise and confusion of a crowded base lodge to eat or use the toilet?

Is the ski learning center in close proximity to the indoor play area? Is it protected by location or fencing from older skiers whizzing through? What type of "lift" is there for the children to get to the top of the learn-ing hill? Many areas use a slow-moving rope tow, though increasingly popular is the "endless belt" developed at Vail. The belt is about 3 feet wide and a couple hundred feet long. Youngsters simply stand on it in their skis at the bottom of the slope and ride to the top. It's sort of like moving stairs.

Once the children are ready to head out of the learning center and onto the mountain, is there a handy novice area—with green trails and a slow-traveling chairlift or detachable quad—for all beginners, from youngsters to seniors?

Ask about the qualifications of the instructors. For the most part instructors at top-quality ski schools—whether in a small gem or a major destination resort—have had special training in working with children. Many also are certified.

Finally, know what the cost of the ski school covers. Are rental boots and skis, as well as lunch with the instructor, included, or is there an additional charge for them?

A Bit of Togetherness

Ski schools generally start lessons about an hour after the lifts begin running. Classes typically end an hour or so before the lifts grind to a halt. Take advantage of these two open hours to be with your ski-schooler.

Togetherness in the morning provides a wonderful opportunity to admire your child, to soothe any fears or uncomfortable feelings she may have about leaving Mom and Dad to join a ski class—especially for the first couple days at a new ski resort—and to spend a cheerful hour skiing before the class meets.

Children bond swiftly in a ski class. By the third day your child will probably be eager to join her classmates. She may act as though they're lifelong friends. And they're sharing an experience, sharing a joy, sharing each other.

Ski schools should keep the four- to eight-year-old ski bunnies in a protected area after their lessons end and until their parents arrive. If your children are like ours were, they'll be impatiently anxious to take a last run with you and show you how much they learned in class that day.

They'll also be overflowing with tidbits about what happened in class: who fell, who bumped into whom, what the instructor said.

There was only one occasion, when our twins were all of six, that I ignored my own advice about skiing with the kids before and after lessons.

It was because of the nefarious way the ski school at Chamonix, in the dramatic French Alps, operated. For the parents who wished, a little van arrived around 8 A.M. to gather the bundled-up young skiers and their gear from in front of their condos and drive them to the ski school for a cup of hot chocolate before heading for the slopes. For parents not on hand to welcome their children from the runs in the afternoon, the school drove them back to their condos at precisely 5 P.M.

We yielded to the gross temptation of missing our traditional one-hour, late-afternoon ski with the girls one day. Mommy and Dad succumbed to laziness.

Scrambling from the ski school van in front of our snow-covered condo that afternoon, the twins made no effort to hide their unhappiness over our absence when they'd skied down from the mountain to find us not waiting anxiously for a final run together. To soothe their hackles we set off for a walk along the snowy streets to a portable sidewalk stand shaded by an awesome green umbrella. Under it a cheerful young French chef, eyes sparkling, was cooking delicate crêpes whose irresistible odor filled the evening air. Mom and Dad had theirs sprinkled with sugar and cognac. For the girls, a gooey chocolate filling.

They sort of forgave us.

An Important Talk

I've never met an instructor who wasn't eager to tell parents how, and what, their young skiers were learning; to describe what the school expected of the kids in the class; and to offer individual suggestions for helping their young ones when skiing with them on the mountain.

While skiing parents are seemingly incapable of skiing with their kids without correcting technical flaws, I implore you to resist this temptation until you've had an opportunity to chat with their instructor. Techniques change. Children are taught at a different pace than adults. Even if you recognize problems that you feel you can solve while on the mountain, go easy on your children and yourself until you've had that personal talk.

How Long Should Lessons Continue?

Look at this way: Olympic skiers and world-class racers have to be among the finest skiers on any slopes, at any place, at any time. Do they need, in effect, lessons? Well, they always work with a coach. Or, to put it another way, they never stop taking lessons.

To maintain, or improve, our own skills, neither you nor I are so damn good we don't need an occasional lesson.

Our policy, until they were almost teenagers, was to enroll Hilary and Rebecca in a ski school anytime we were on a weeklong play-the-mountain holiday—even when their skill level reached from high intermediate to low expert.

Grouped only with other strong skiers, they found the classes genuinely challenging, and were always picking up helpful hints on technique, whether for bouncing down the bumps on a black run or carving turns on powder. Since young skiers of these skill levels rarely continue to go to ski school, the girls' classes were inevitably small; this, of course, gave the instructors the opportunity to fine-tune the weaknesses of each skier. And another plus: The girls quickly developed new friends with whom they'd prefer to ski than with their rather old-fogy parents.

When they reached their teens we shifted our focus onto lessons, offering them, instead, an occasional couple hours' skiing with a private instructor if they wanted it. They never let us save a penny by turning the offer down.

After only a few years of skiing these two redheads could keep up with anything Gail or I could handle. And by the time they were 12—as I recounted—I heard the saddest words on the mountain.

Mountain Manners

However, the fact that they did spend time in various ski schools did not eliminate what I feel keenly is the responsibility of all parents of kids on the mountain—the teaching of manners and safety.

We tried to instill in our daughters such habits as never stopping where other skiers couldn't easily see them; not skiing, or stopping, too close to others; never deliberately schussing down the trail at speeds beyond their ability to control; avoiding skiers below them; being patient in lift lines; offering a helping hand to any skier having special problems or involved in an accident.

Very early in their ski years we also taught them what the various signs meant—the green, blue, and black markers, TRAIL CLOSED, and DAN-GER, among others. Once they reached an age where they could understand trail maps, we played a special game: "Getting From Here to There." My wife or I would suddenly hand the girls a map and say, in effect, "We're lost. Can you find on the map where we are?"

Once they found the spot, we'd point to another trail and say, "You've got to get us over there. You've got the map."

Eventually—sometimes with a bit of judicious help—they'd lead us to the new trail. By the time they were eight map reading was old hat to these redheads, who actually never wore hats—unless the weather was brutal and their mom insisted.

SKIS, BOOTS, BINDINGS
Renting

Unless you have the good fortune to possess a fortune, there's no need to spend a fortune on skis, boots, and bindings for those fast-growing children, especially for total beginners or those who may ski only a few days each winter. So, let's first talk rentals.

The first skis for children in the three-to-five or -six bracket are usually available as separate rentals, or included with the fee, for those who enter ski school. If you must rent equipment outside the school, always inspect the skis as carefully as you would those you rent for yourself. Don't worry about the cosmetics. Are the edges sharp? Are the bottoms smooth and without major gouges?

Properly adjusted bindings are as important for the young skier as for her grandmother. To test whether he's properly adjusted the bindings, the attendant fitting the boot to the binding will usually simply give the boot a sharp blow to knock it out of the binding. For the lightweights who tip the scale at less than 50 pounds this test is quite satisfactory, though it's also a wise precaution for Mom or Dad to check the bindings while still in the rental shop. Have the child step into the bindings then lean hard, and far, forward, pulling up her heels, to make certain the heel doesn't pop out. Then try twisting her boots out of the bindings. Everything still attached? Pick up the skis and weave through the crowds into the fresh air. The mountain beckons.

Rental boots seldom fit as comfortably as a child's own, but look them over, especially the toe and bottom of the heel. Avoid those that are worn away on those two vital places, because wear and tear there complicate proper release of the bindings. Always have your child wear his warmest ski socks when trying on the boots—which should fit snugly but not tightly. You should be able to put a finger inside the boot behind the child's heel before the boots are snapped closed. Overly tight boots will impede blood circulation, which means only one thing: "Mommy, my feet are cold."

Boots should be loosened for the ride up on the chairlift to help the blood circulate in the feet. (Loosen yours, too.)

Buying

Whatever you buy for a child today will be too small next year.

There are several ways to reduce the credit card cramps that come from buying everything new each season:

If your children will ski only a few days each winter, keep on renting.

However, if skiing is definitely a family preoccupation, consider seasonal rentals. Increasingly popular is a plan that allows parents to rent new equipment for an entire season then, for a reasonable fee, buy the skis and boots when the winter ends.

If you're buying used boots, skis, and bindings, there's only one good source: a reputable ski shop that not only sells its rentals from last season, but also has the facilities to repair and test them.

Be cautious, and dubious, about buying from friends or at used-ski sales. Always have used equipment checked by an expert, even if it's a hand-me-down that big brother used a couple years ago. A good ski shop will do this, though it may charge a small fee.

Bindings, whether new or used, must be carefully adjusted for the child's weight and skiing level. Since a youngster can move from a nervous green-slope skier to a sturdy skier on the blues, plus add a couple inches and a chunk of pounds, in one season, bindings should be recalibrated about midway through the winter.

Inevitably, questions arise about the quality, length, and type of ski to buy for a growing child, or the safety of a particular binding. Not too many years ago quality was a major concern, because few manufacturers produced anything for children but what could best be described as cosmetically attractive junk. Today there's no need for even a hint of concern about the quality of boots, bindings, and skis.

However, you and the youngster alike may wonder whether you should buy a ski with a soft or firm flex, and how long it should be. While it's simple to come up with formulas—soft-flex skis 6 inches longer than the child is tall for the novice, or kid bindings until a youngster weighs 75 pounds—these are, at best, semiguesses. Go to the experts for advice: ski school instructors or the experienced personnel at a reputable ski shop, whether at the resort or in your home town.

When buying, heed the advice you'll find in annual summaries of new skis, boots, and bindings for kids in the major ski publications.

Finally, there's the question whether or not young skiers should wear helmets. The obvious answer is: Of course. But what's not quite so obvious is that medical experts aren't convinced that helmets help, or hurt. As one medical authority expressed it: If a youngster suffers an accident involving his or her head, a helmet can prevent major injury. Another, however, had a warning: Large-sized helmets obscure the child's vision and can end up causing more injuries than they prevent.

Because of these concerns, helmet manufacturers are now designing thinner helmets that more closely approximate the size of the head.

My opinion: Buy them, especially if your child is an aggressive skier or a racer. But buy the newest, thin models.

Keeping 'Em Comfortable

No parent needs to be reminded that youngsters must be warmly bundled against cold, wind, and snow. On the other hand, kids don't have to be so swaddled in piles of winter clothing that they can't even waddle, much less ski or frolic, in the out-of-doors.

So the proper way to dress a child for skiing is to recognize both factors. Dress her just enough to keep her comfortable. Overdressing is as awkward a mistake as is taking her to ski school inadequately clothed for a whole day on the slopes.

The principle of layering holds true for the youngster as well as for Mom and Dad. A well-layered young skier dons long johns, then a turtleneck to protect the neck, a sweater to go over the turtleneck, and finally a top-quality ski outfit, either pants and coat or a single-piece. Add a neck gaiter that can be pulled up to a sniffling nose on zero days, a warm cap with earflaps, mittens, and socks. Layers can be added or subtracted as the weather and comfort dictate.

Now, let's look at some specifics:

Long johns: The new polypropylene fabrics are as effective in keeping children warm and dry as adults.

Mittens: Never gloves. Buy only water-resistant models, such as those with an outer layer of Gore-Tex, which lets moisture escape but keeps out the wet. Don't stint on quality. Little hands deserve the best. Of course, tie the mittens onto the sleeves so they won't disappear in the cloakroom.

Socks: Only, but only, thick socks made especially for skiers. The fabric may range from sturdy wool to man-made fibers.

Cap: Up to 50 percent of all body heat is lost through the head alone. Cover it up. A warm hat with earflaps becomes increasingly important as temperatures drop. Avoid cutesy caps with long tops that project 2 to 4 feet. The tops can easily get tangled on a lift. In fact, some lift operators require skiers to remove long, flapping caps before boarding.

Ski goggles: These are essential. Accept nothing less than goggles that protect against UVA and UVB ultraviolet rays.

Sunscreen lotion: Use one with an SPF of at least 15 at lower-elevation ski resorts; at least 25 when you're skiing more than 7,000 feet above sea level.

Headband: Girls love to wear these. It holds the hair in place. Not for cold weather.

Ski outfit: The outer fabric must be reasonably water resistant, and the garment should be stuffed with only a top-rated man-made fabric or down with a fill rating of no less than 550. Do not waste money on a "down and feather" filling or a down that doesn't specify the fill rating.

For the preschooler, the most suitable outfit is a one-piece garment; this provides the greatest protection during the vigorous outdoor pleasure of learning to ski and frolic in the snow simultaneously. Older kids may go for either a one- or a two-piece outfit. In a two-piece, pants with a bib provide far more comfort than regular pants.

A garment that uses a zipper closure, with a flap to cover the zipper, is warmer than one with buttons.

For very cold and windy days, everyone appreciates an inner polypro felt or down vest, or wool sweater, worn over the turtleneck.

Diet

The cold-weather diet that helps maintain an adult's body temperature also works for children. The greatest problem, especially at the breakfast table, is to keep the youngsters from overstuffing themselves with sugary foods and drinks. Sugar provides a strong burst of energy that quickly dissipates. In other words, kids will be a bundle of warmth for an hour or so after a meal high in sugars; then the cold will set in. Not too smart as a breakfast meal.

Encourage the intake of fats and proteins for the slow-burning fuels that provide day-long warmth. For breakfast, serve the cereals with the lowest sugar content. Read the label on the package. Bacon and sausage are a fine additional source of slow-burning food energy. At lunch that fast-food delicacy, the cheeseburger, and those delicious, greasy french fries provide long-lasting fuel.

Children need extra fluid when they're active outdoors in the winter. Least effective are highly sugared drinks, especially colas with caffeine. Encourage nonsugared fruit juices. Children will suffer chills from even slight dehydration.

A hearty, good-to-slurp soup for dinner increases fluid intake.

Satisfy any craving for sugar by bringing out rich desserts, chock-ablock with heavy cream and chocolate. And of course, a good-night cup of whole-milk hot chocolate is a healthy and cheerful send-off to bed.

Nonskiing Necessities

Après-ski boots: These are an important adjunct on a ski trip. The best are those that slip on quickly and are both warm and tolerably lightweight. Laceup boots are a foolish no-no for the very young.

Lightweight parka: This can replace the regular ski jacket on a two-piece suit on warm days. It's also a fine substitute for a raincoat when the snow falls in round droplets.

Warming chemicals: Buy ones small enough to fit inside mittens and boots—they're an instant solution to tearful complaints about cold hands and feet. Carry a couple sets for each child.

Ankle gaiters: These are excellent at keeping snow from soaking into boots. The inner linings of boots, however, usually do get damp. Remember, inner linings can be removed at night for drying.

Lock: Children's skis do get stolen—chiefly shiny new skis. If the youngster has her own she should also have an inexpensive lock to fasten them to the ski rack outside the lodge.

Boot bags: These are not an option but a necessity. Children will be far happier with their own than grumpily sharing with a sibling or with the parents. I know ours were, even in their younger years. Not only should their bag hold their ski boots, it should also hold the nonclothing necessities that go on every cheerful ski junket: mittens, goggles, moisture-proofing cloth for the goggles, hat, sunscreen, ski lock, neck and ankle gaiters, and any can't-do-without personal articles.

Kids usually outgrow their clothes and equipment before it wears out. To insure that a hand-me-down ski outfit is water resistant spray lightly with a water-repellent for fabric. Worn inner ski boot linings are replaceable. Have a younger sibling's skis inspected by a skilled mechanic before passing them on from an older brother or sister. They should be checked to make sure they have not gotten warped over the years and the bindings cleaned and calibrated for the weight and ski level of their new owner.

Each of our two daughters is personally responsible for seeing that all equipment that returns from a ski trip is properly stored. Boots are cleaned, dried, and packed into the ski bag, along with the other accessories. Skis are wiped down with a lightly oiled cloth before being stored. That all accomplished, everything is in order for the next adventure.

7

Other Snow Seekers

There are those who do it differently. One example: Extreme. These skiers are featured in Warren Miller movies leaping off cliffs, skiing the wildest terrain, and challenging the meanest slopes on the mountains. Learn about the schools that teach these unbelievable techniques. Snowboarding is also becoming a more significant part of skiing every winter. Some resorts restrict snowboarders, but find out why the trails and snowboard parks are almost everywhere, and pick up a hint or two on how to learn the basics yourself. As for cross-country, it's a wonderful sport whether practiced on a snowy golf course or on the increasing number of groomed trails maintained by resorts, for the off-slope skiers.

EXTREME

We've all gasped at pictures of skiers leaping off cliffs, plunging down snowy bluffs, hurtling between rocks from one patch of snow to another, or skiing a gradient so steep it's impossible for any human to survive. But they're doing it.

Who? The extreme skiers.

Of course, we seldom see personally those skiers ignoring all the laws of gravity to ski the unbelievable, because these fearless, death-defying gladiators of the snows who challenge the meanest, steepest, most dangerous grades on any mountain are away "off piste," far beyond the trails, glades, and bowls where intelligent skiers enjoy the challenge of the slopes without being idiotic enough to toy with suicide. Yet there are

An extreme skier leaps off a challenging cliff at Sugarbush, Vermont.

skiers whose blood rushes at the merest hint they might somehow, some-where, someday leap off those same cliffs and scream in delirious joy racing down those same drops.

If perchance—and it is conceivable—you're one of the feverish few who wishes to learn the techniques and skills of skiing beyond reality, you can. It's done through a group of relatively new Ski Schools for the Gloriously Mad.

Among the most prominent is The Extreme Team. It holds advanced clinics every winter at a few ski resorts, eastern and western, including Bolton Valley/Sugarbush; Grand Targhee, Wyoming (the winter home of The Extreme Team); Lake Louise, Alberta; Crested Butte; Squaw Valley; and Whistler/Blackcomb, British Columbia.

The seven instructors of The Extreme Team clinic in the mid-1990s are some of the most dynamic skiers in the world. There are two sets of brothers. You may have seen one pair, Jon and Dan Egan, in Warren Miller's ski movie *Extreme Winter*. In the opening sequence, filmed at Grand Targhee, the two are beginning a steep run when sud-denly a 3-ton cornice breaks under their feet. Only by leaping and turning in midair do the brothers save their lives and produce a gut-clutching moment in a ski movie. The two make their winter home at Grand Targhee.

The other brothers are Rob and Eric DesLauriers. Both spent years making extreme skiing movies and competing as extreme skiers before largely taking the leadership in creating The Extreme Team.

Two women leap into the air, hurtling down to the snowy slopes. Want to join them? Or let them instruct you in how it's done? They are Kristen Ulmer, who says the way to ski extreme is to be aggressive, and Kristen Lignell, whose favorite concept is smoothness.

Dean Decas, who spent years teaching high-speed bump, or mogul, skiing techniques and six years as an extreme instructor, is the seventh Extreme Team member.

Private Practice

Those eager to work out with an Extreme Team clinic should heed Dan Egan's Golden Rule: "Ski the mountain, don't let the mountain ski you." Here's his advice regarding private ski practice that will help aggressive experts learn the basics of extreme skiing:

"Skiing is a constant realignment of balance. As an advanced skier you must learn to adapt to the changing terrain and snow conditions. Be aggressive and consistent no matter what you are skiing.

"Start by skiing at a consistent speed at all times. Establish a speed you are comfortable with, but one in which you are in control and can stop or change direction in a split second.

"Once you've established your 'comfort speed,' ski constantly changing terrain. Ski directly into every trail without stopping at the top. This is excellent to learn to adapt speed and technique to all terrain.

"Challenge yourself. Ski off the lift and onto a favorite trail without stopping. Try making fifty turns the same radius and at the same speed, or mix the radius of your turns but always at the same speed.

"Skiing changing terrain and adapting while in motion will be the best teachers for your mind and body. The mountain will become less intimidating. You'll be skiing things you never thought possible."

Dan's advice is for both men and women. And this is just fine with Kristen Ulmer. She says there are a variety of reasons women join extreme ski clinics: "Some women want to ski their first black diamond, others want to try cliff jumps or radical ski mountaineering. Either way, there's nothing finer than a woman discovering her power as an athlete.

"Women can go as extreme as men anytime. It's just a mind-set to go for it."

Extreme Clinic

An Extreme Team clinic follows this general pattern:

First morning: Ski the blacks and double blacks. Not hard, you know. This is not only to show off your skills but also to help instructors group you with others at your level.

First afternoon: Ski on and off groomed runs to learn the basics of carving turns on steep terrain while finding what Dan refers to as a "balanced center on the ski, [a] focus on using the whole ski to do the work." Getting a bit tougher.

Second morning: The objective here is "visualization," which involves skiing both on and off double-black runs, at sustained high speeds, to gain an inner sense of the ultimate that extreme skiing demands.

Second afternoon: More and more demanding. Searching for all different snow conditions and exposure to such little handicaps as rocks, trees, and chutes. Learning specific techniques for those conditions. Now it's damned tough.

Third morning: Take to the air. Shoot off the moguls. Leap from 10, 20, 30 feet. Ski everywhere.

Third afternoon: Search it out. Tear it up. Explore the toughest that the mountain has to offer and that you have to give.

Third evening: Every man and woman who's survived these three days gets an award at a noisy, exuberant, "we-made-it-alive" celebration.

Want to join them?

For further information, contact: Extreme Team Advanced Ski Clinics, P.O. Box 368, Crested Butte, CO 81224; or Grand Targhee, Extreme Team, Box Ski, Alta, WY 83422. Or check with your favorite resort. It now may be offering special programs for extreme skiers.

SNOWBOARDMANIA

Snowboarding, despite the widespread illusion that it's a wild sport indulged in only by wild-eyed teenagers hurtling wildly down mountains without sense or control, is actually a civilized and challenging winter pastime that's an integral part of today's ski scene. It has nothing to do with age, or attitude.

Teenagers snowboard. So do riders in their 50s. It was once an almost exclusively male sport, but at least 15 percent of the boarders swooping and pivoting down the slopes today are women. It's estimated that about one third of boarders are also skiers. Burton Snowboards, which has been manufacturing snowboards since the late 1970s, estimates that 12 percent of the tickets sold at mountain resorts in the winter of 1994–95 were for snowboarders. The percentage is edging up annually.

Snowboarders, and the special industry that serves them, fight desperately to maintain the aura of being, well, different. Look, for example, at this ad by Burton in *Powder* magazine. It captures the freaky spirit of the snowboard universe:

SNOWBOARDING IS NOT:

Extreme or rad.

Olympic-hopeful or anti-hero.

Allowed at Sundance or banned at Huntah.

Eating buffalo wings in the lodge or spitting off the lift.
Wearing tennis bracelets or nipple rings.
Skin-tight or XXXL.
IT'S YOU, SCUM.

Fundamentally, say the boarders, we are the exciting next generation of alpine skiing, pursuing a new snow sport that, as one aficionado described it, is "totally geared for descent."

Snowboarding was begun in the United States in the last 1960s by ocean surfers trying to figure out what they could do on oversized skateboards on the snow. Today it involves equipment as sophisticated as the most modern skis, boots, and bindings. Its popularity has spread from the hills and dales of American resorts to ski areas around the world.

Ten years ago only a handful of ski resorts were brave enough to permit snowboarders to charge, loop, fly, and carve down their slopes. Today, only a handful of resorts, some major, some small, ban them. It's smart, of course, for snowboarders heading for a new area to call ahead and make certain their boards are welcome.

When the Winter Olympics are held on the snowy slopes of Utah in 2002, snowboarding competition will be included for the first time.

One manager of a major resort that admits snowboarders says many skiers complain about the attitude of snowboarders, accusing them of a disregard for the etiquette of skiing, being reckless on the mountain, cutting lift lines, and foul language.

At Wildcat Mountain in New Hampshire, a spokesman says he feels problems with snowboarders are "overstated," because "they wear baggy clothing, have their own slang, and come across as being different."

Both to woo snowboarders and to give them an area on the mountain away from the general ski runs many areas have created special parks with man-made artifices specifically for snowboarders. The obstacles have such names as tabletops, spines, rail slides, and the increasingly familiar half-pipes—rounded trenches from 400 to 700 feet long in which skilled boarders swoop from side to side, flipping in aerial turns, awing spectators, and having one helluva great time.

And, quite naturally, there are snowboard schools for everyone from the never-evers eager to learn to experts who want to improve their jumps, spins, and flips.

This is the way the experts snowboard.

Just how popular is snowboarding on the snowy slopes? The National Sporting Goods Association estimates that there were 2.1 million snowboarders in 1994–95—compared with 1.5 million a year earlier—and forecasts 2.3 million for the 1995–96 season.

Ski Industries of America estimates that 187,000 snowboards were sold in the United States in 1994, up 8 percent from the previous year.

While the number of snowboarders, especially in the under-21 set, has soared in the past few years, at the same time total daily attendance at ski resorts has edged up only slightly, suggesting that snowboarders are not ski enthusiasts trying out new equipment but younger skiers who've opted for the single board rather than a pair of sticks.

Getting Started

For those interested in sampling snowboarding, the same rules apply as in skiing. Rent the gear. You can practice the basic elements by yourself, but to become proficient after that you'll need to take lessons.

Rental shops generally offer beginners an all-mountain, or freestyle board with an easy flex and a slightly tipped-up nose and tail. The average length for men is from 150 to 170 cm; for women, 140 to 160 cm. Rental shops usually recommend chin height for newcomers.

Beginners will find it easier to learn how to handle the stubborn boards if they start out in soft boots, but avoid those that are extremely low cut. Some snowboard instructors also recommend boots with the extra support of stiff overlaps. Make certain rental boots fit snugly and hold your heel firmly.

Snowboarders can also wear specifically designed hard boots. These are similar in appearance to regular plastic ski boots, but the two are not interchangeable. Riders' boots curve up at the toe and heel so they won't drag in the snow.

As for bindings, the most popular for beginners are the two-strap high-back models, which give added support behind the leg. Traditionally, each binding is snapped on individually, though a step-in binding—a blessing skiers have long enjoyed—is now under development.

The First Lesson

Not anxious to spend the bucks for a snowboarder's sloppy clothing until I became a confirmed boarder, I showed up with rented gear, wearing my normal ski outfit, for my first snowboard lesson in the bright sunshine of a perfect ski day at Wachusetts, a gem of a ski area in Massachusetts. The instructor, a pert and enthusiastic young woman named April, asked me if I were "regular" or "goofy"—snowboardese for which foot I placed forward.

"Does it make any difference?" I asked.

"Oh, yes," she replied. "A great deal. It's the difference between snowboarding and falling all over the snow."

She explained that one method of figuring out which foot goes first is to have someone behind you give you a sudden push forward. The foot that you extend to keep from falling over is the foot that should go in the forward binding. Almost as soon as she gave me this explanation, I was suddenly shoved from behind. I threw my left foot forward to stay erect.

Another tecnhique is to run and slide on a slippery surface. Whichever foot leads is the one that goes in front.

"Regular," it turned out, is the right foot forward; "goofy," the left.

Our first lesson began at the flat area in front of the base lodge when our class of four jovial women and two tall and slender young men, all in their early 20s, and yours truly, a gray-haired somewhere-over-the-distant-40s, locked our lead boots into our front bindings and looped straps to one ankle as a safety precaution for beginners. Boards don't have runaway brakes to keep them from scooting off by themselves. The bindings don't release.

Then April had us stand so that our feet were semi-sideways, one in the binding and one in the snow. We were facing forward keeping our weight centered and our knees bent, with one hand extended to each side of the board.

"Okay," she called out, "use your free foot to push yourself slowly. If you push too hard the board may shoot out from under you. Keep your free foot close to the snowboard. Practice pushing in gentle steps to gain a sense of balance."

We started to move in a wide circle. Only two of us beginners didn't experience the awkward embarrassment of ending up on the snow.

Once we began to feel comfortable carefully shoving our way along, we learned how to glide.

"Push with your free foot. When you start to move, place your free foot on the board and against the back binding and glide," shouted April.

We practiced gliding on the flat snow. Push with the rear foot. Place the foot on the board. Glide.

Eventually satisfied that we'd learned, if somewhat haltingly, how to glide, we were lined up for our first effort at snowboarding down an easy slope.

We edged onto the slope, maneuvering our snowboards so they were at right angles to the fall line. Then, locking our free feet into the back bindings, we tilted the snowboards downhill and, lo, began to slide down.

April warned us to keep equal pressure on both feet as we slipped down the fall line, and to keep our knees bent and the board at a right angle to the slope. To slow our speed, we were told to push down on our heels so that the back edge of the board dug into the snow. To go a bit faster, we leaned slightly forward, pushing down on our toes.

Amazing! Hey, maybe this will become my new sport, I thought.

Next came the "falling leaf," a maneuver in which we moved our boards to the left or right in a sort of zigzag motion without really turning. As we started sliding down the fall line, our boards again at a right angle to the slope, we were told to look to the right and shift our weight gently to the right foot. Even more amazing. My board actually began to slide to the right.

To move to the left, the procedure was exactly the same: Look to the left, shift your weight to the left foot, and the board will edge to the left.

April, obviously showing off by snowboarding backwards so she could keep a wary eye on all of us, warned: "As you move back and forth put pressure on the back edge to slow down so the boards don't run away with you."

For me, her warning came a split second too late.

I quickly discovered that getting up from a fall on a slope is as challenging to the snowboarder as it is to the skier. If you fall facing uphill, keep your board at a right angle to the fall line, roll over onto your knees, dig your board's uphill edge into the snow, get onto your knees, and push yourself up.

The finale of that first lesson was to learn to convert the falling leaf into a linked turn.

Under our instructor's sharp eye, we started by actually pointing our boards down the fall line, sort of, and looking in the direction we wanted to turn.

As she explained: To turn to the heel side, look to the heel side, push down easily on your heels, and the board will begin turning to the heel side. After it turns, look to the toe side, and your board will begin to follow your eyes. As it moves slowly to the toe side, shift your weight slightly to your toes, to ease the pressure on the back of the board while it's turning.

It worked. Look to the toe side, turn to the toe side; look to the heel side, turn to the heel side.

What pleasant, if slow-motion, excitement, interrupted only occasionally by all of us individually practicing getting up from the snow.

Class over. Now we were free to practice what we'd learned. Falling leaf glide. Getting up. Easy linked turns. Falling. Getting up. More turns.

For novice snowboarders who achieve this elemental level of linked turns, doing it with speed and élan will come far more quickly if they take a few more lessons. After that, the half-pipe!

Or, for me, back to the skis.

Clothing

Boarders' outfits have a sort of grunge look. Loose, almost sloppy. This is not a matter of smart-ass styling. It's simply one of being suited for the occasion. The loose fit is essential because snowboarding involves a lot more twisting and turning and bending than regular skiing does.

Since riders frequently drag their hands in the snow, their gloves need to be well reinforced and have long cuffs to keep out the snow.

The rider's parka has reinforced side panels—designed to protect the garment when the snowboard is carried. It's also longer in the back than a regular parka, or has a drop seat to protect the butt from the snow.

The jeans are huge and insulated, with reinforcement on the seat and the knees—also for protection when falling, sitting, or kneeling on the snow.

Boarders also wear $10 imitation Arnet sunglasses, and "beanies"—snowboardese for those goofy-looking, extra-tall watch caps—and they talk in their own private code about such things as "fat air," or a "sick quarter-pipe," or "hucking your puck," which clearly doesn't ingratiate them to the, well, established skiers.

But if their hip-hop attitude offends some, when the expert snowboarders take off on their wild maneuvers, doing a mute, a lein, or a nuclear stiffy, spinning through space like tops, sailing off cliffs at speeds that are almost frightening to watch, they win deep respect for their daring and skill.

CROSS-COUNTRY

The ancient grandfather of alpine skiing, cross-country skiing, is alive, healthy, and more popular than at any time in his 4,000-year history.

True, no longer do sturdy Vikings lash their fur boots to 10-foot-long slabs of wood with upturned points to travel snowy stretches of the winter countryside. Today, their descendants, like good cross-country skiers everywhere, don the proper clothing, slip their feet into low-cut special shoes that fasten by the tip into a binding that allows the heel to move up and down freely, and traverse hill and glade. And, even as they do in Idaho's snow-clad mountains, or across New York City's Central Park when it's adrift in white, cross-country skiers enjoy the glory days of winter.

There's one significant difference between cross-country—or, as it's sometimes spelled, x-country—skiing and the alpine kind. Work! In alpine skiing, there's a lift to carry you to the summit. Gravity pulls you down. In cross-country, you do it yourself. You propel yourself on the flats. You push your way uphill.

But cross-country has some attractive advantages over alpine. The equipment is simpler, easier to learn to use, and far less expensive than the complex boots and bindings the alpine enthusiast wears. Cross-country devotees can ski all they want through the virgin snows without paying a penny for enjoying park, woodland, or prairie. However, the enthusiast quickly learns that skiing maintained trails at ski resorts is an easier and more pleasurable way to enjoy the sport than plowing through deep snow, even as his fellow alpine skier knows it's more pleasurable to ride a lift to the summit than to hike up with his skis on his back. And for those who forsake the woods for the groomed runs there is, of course, a fee.

Increasingly, alpine ski areas are adding kilometers of trails (in x-country skiing you travel kilometers, not miles) groomed for the two basic styles of cross-country skiing—touring and skating. For touring, a grooming machine smoothes two parallel tracks. Cross-country skiers merely ski in the tracks. The skating trail is a groomed, wide lane for cross-country skiers who ski as though they were ice skating. The ski-skating system was developed by cross-country racers in Europe. It's more difficult to learn than the touring technique but, quite naturally, skating is the style used today in cross-country racing.

Equipment

First-timers can rent cross-country skis and shoes at the ski resorts that maintain trails, as well as at many ski shops. However, cross-country skis, poles, and shoes are relatively low priced compared to alpine equipment. It makes good dollar sense to buy your own equipment.

The cross-country shoe looks somewhat like a modern running shoe, with a sole that extends an inch or so forward of the toe. There are three holes in the extension. The binding is little more than a hinged toepiece with three upright pins. The three pins in the tip of the binding are inserted into the holes in the shoe, and the binding snapped shut. A sole grip is attached to the ski to guide the heel as it rises and falls.

A slightly different shoe is the push-button model. This boot's narrower and extended toepiece has a single hole, which the single pin in the binding slides into. Manufacturers say the extended toepiece in the push-button enables the skier to lift the heel higher, thus permitting her to take longer strides.

Within the past 20 years, fiberglass skis have begun to replace wooden models. They do have certain advantages over the wood. They're stronger, more durable, and easier to both to learn on and to use, especially the new breed of "nonwax" skis with a base that has a sort of fish-scale or curbed-step pattern. The ski slides forward easily, but the patterned base prevents it from sliding backward. This design is based on that of the traditional ski, in which special skins were attached to the base, with the hairs sloping backward. When the skier glided forward, the hairs laid back. On uphill climbs, the hairs, like the patterned fiberglass base, prevented the ski from sliding backward.

Wood or fiberglass, all smooth-base skis need wax, and patterned fiberglass bases also work better when waxed. There are a variety of waxes for a variety of snow conditions, temperature ranges, and ski usages. However, the average recreational skier will find two waxes to be adequate: a soft, or "plus," wax for temperatures above zero, and a hard or "minus" wax when the temperatures drop below zero.

Long and strong is the description for cross-country poles, because they're used to push the skier along. The usual standard of measurement is that the pole should reach up to your armpit.

Beginning Techniques

When my family suddenly made a joint decision to take up cross-country skiing none of us really knew anything more about the sport than that we could do it 50 yards from our Upper West Side Manhattan brownstone in nearby Riverside Park, which stretches for miles along the Hudson River. Aha. Now we could whip out of the house and be skiing in five minutes.

The switch from downhill to cross-country was not without its quota of slips and falls, but my two daughters caught on more quickly than my wife or myself. We began under the tutelage of a friend who had once—years before—been an ardent cross-country addict.

Lining us up one brisk Sunday morning when the sun glistened off the snow, he had us put on our skis at the top of a small incline.

"It's easy. Just coast down and when you stop, we'll talk about techniques."

Easy? Quite confusing. These weren't alpine skis, and we found within one minute that they didn't behave like them.

As though we were sensible never-evers on the mountain, we began by learning how to glide forward. Our mentor had us walk slowly, leisurely, sort of half pushing ourselves with our elongated poles. Ah, more like it. The walking turned into a slightly gliding step.

We were fortunate in the amazing number of cross-country skiers in the park. Like the experienced x-country skiers they all seemed to be, they followed someone else's tracks. We did the same. Within the hour we were all doing a sort of forward glide step. Push. Glide. Push. Glide. The glide became longer. The push on the poles firmer. Our steps longer. Our glides longer.

After learning the step-push-glide sequence, we practiced the double-pole push. Simple. Keeping both feet together, we pushed vigorously backward with both poles simultaneously, at the same time leaning slightly forward.

Wearing nonwax skis with fish-scale bottoms, it was relatively easy to walk-step up gentle inclines.

Cross-country skiers on a groomed trail.

Next, we practiced two techniques that every alpine skier must also learn. The first was sidestepping up a hill, keeping our skis at a right angle to the fall line and climbing up sideways. This was followed by the herringbone: spreading the ski tips far apart, keeping the tails close together, and walking straight up the slope.

For both sidestepping and the herringbone it was essential to use the poles for pushing and control.

End day one. Glorious.

Within a few hours we'd gone from total beginners to slightly experienced novices, discovering as we did so why cross-country skiing has attracted millions.

Advanced Techniques

Moving from an easy gliding step to an advanced is akin to going from a brisk walk to a slow run. To perform the advanced gliding step, use a strong push from your thrusting leg, keeping your knees bent so your weight is well forward, and, simultaneously, pushing vigorously with your pole. The glide should be long, with your weight over the gliding ski. Go into your next step as soon as you begin to slow down.

The two most serious mistakes are keeping the weight too far back, so that the rear ski comes down too soon, and keeping the body too stiff, which pushes the body upward rather than forward.

Snowplow turns are exactly the same as what downhill skiers learn to curve their way down the fall line. Wedge your skis into a snowplow, tips together, tails apart. When you place your weight on one ski, you move in the opposite direction. You travel by shifting your weight from one ski to the other.

Cross-country skiers can also use easy stem and parallel turns. These are difficult to control because the skis are slender and have no metal edges. X-country boots are light on the foot, and the bindings don't hold the boot tightly, so your foot won't always go where you aim it. Practice is the answer.

The ultimate x-country ski turn is the telemark. Those with the skill and control to use the telemark are the "skinny skiers" you watch carving their way down any groomed pitch at a ski resort, from green to double black, while you ride the lift to the summit.

In the telemark, the skier adopts a sort of kneeling position when turning, the outside ski leading and the inside ski, with the knee deeply bent, following.

The skis used in telemark skiing are similar to cross-country but have metal edges, which makes them easier to control on alpine runs and difficult off-slope terrain.

Clothing

Remember, x-country is work along with fun. And work means working up a sweat. To stay comfortable when pushing and puffing across snowy countryside, dress casually and in layers.

Knickers, which snap just below the knee, are an excellent way to keep from overheating. Otherwise, wear a pair of warm, but not heavy, pants. Ankle gaiters will keep the snow out of your shoes and prevent it from piling up under your pant legs. If you don't have gaiters, wrap your pant cuffs around your ankles and stuff the cuffs inside your socks. Long johns are only needed on brutally cold days.

A satisfactory cross-country outfit would include a T-shirt-style undershirt and a warm polypro or wool shirt, with a collar, which can be unbuttoned when you start to sweat. A light jacket with a removable lining, or a down-filled vest, is usually more than sufficient for the cross-country devotee. Adding a cap that can be pulled down over the ears and forehead if the weather turns nasty, and light, water-resistant gloves will just about complete your x-country outfit.

One piece of equipment popular with cross-country travelers is a small waterproof backpack in which to stuff extra socks, a piece of clothing, a thermos of hot soup or coffee, and—if it's going to be a long day—extra water. Dehydration can be a major problem, especially when you're cross-country cruising at high altitudes. And don't forget two other items essential for all skiers: sunglasses and sunscreen lotion.

Where to Ski

When there are only minor slopes, a beginner can have as much fun cross-country skiing parks, fields, and golf courses as any expert. However, remember that unless you're skiing a wide-groomed run, you generally ski in someone else's tracks. You'll find groomed cross-country runs now at almost all destination resorts—as well as many of the small gems—far more enjoyable. Not only do these resorts rent a variety of x-country skis for different skill levels, but their ski shop staffs are also generally happy to talk to you about the proper wax to use for any given snow and weather conditions on a particular day.

Like downhill trails, the cross-country runs at resorts are excellently maintained and marked as to their type and degree of difficulty.

One of the special ski resorts for the cross-country set is Lake Placid, in New York's Adirondacks, where America's Olympic hopefuls in every winter sport—including cross-country skiing—train. There are five Olympic x-country training trails, ranging from easy green to ferocious black. Open to the public, the training area is quite a place to prove how skillful you may, or may not, have become since you first popped your toes into the bindings.

Ski Fest

A highlight of the cross-country season is the annual Ski Fest in early January, when more than 100 ski areas in 22 states and three Canadian provinces offer special incentives for first-time skiers. These include free introductory lessons, discount trail passes, and reduced-fee or free rentals. For information on locations, call Ski Fest at (603) 239-8888.

8

Where to Ski

The numerous books, ski magazines, and feature articles on skiing available today seemingly contain all the information you need to pass advance judgment on a ski resort before riding its lifts. But keep this in mind: The Ski Scene is *different*. And here is why neither skiing the snowy slopes of the Rockies nor the snow-covered Appalachians—neither East nor West—is "superior" for a terrific ski holiday. "Skiing the Gems" explains how a little ski area can be a big bargain. Finally, this section highlights a baker's (or *skier's*) dozen major ski areas and individual resorts in North America, each with its own special aura. These are singled out not because you'll enjoy skiing them any more than a hundred other resorts, but because you might find it interesting simply to know what gives each its unique flavor.

EAST AND WEST
"Oh, east is east and west is west, and never the twain shall meet," sang Rudyard Kipling.

Ski resorts still sting this refrain. But in reality, after skiing the mountains east and the mountains west for more than two decades, I find more similarities than dissimilarities.

Of course, there *are* distinctions. I always know when I'm skiing the slopes of Telluride in Colorado, or Sunday River in Maine. There's not a dramatic difference in the skiing—but there certainly is in the scenery.

Eastern skiers weave their way down the rolling, forested Appalachians. In the West, the spectacular Rockies are the background for great ski runs.

There are other distinctions.

Most western resorts are anchored in a base town. The opposite is true in the East, where ski areas generally developed on suitable mountains with the nearest town anywhere from a few to a dozen miles away. However, whether eastern or western, all destination resorts now have extensive facilities at the base, including both on- and off-slope housing and a variety of shops, bars, and restaurants.

I find a decided appeal in the endeavor of many western resorts to maintain the traditions and mementos of their history. It's fascinating to wander through the streets of Jackson, Wyoming, or Price, Utah, after a day on the slopes and discover that the Old West has been kept alive with original buildings protected as landmarks and the re-created saloons, ancient mine shafts, and other memorials of the past. Or to watch real-life cowboys combine skiing and saddling horses in a rip-snortin', Wild West race at Steamboat Springs. Or to admire the cowboy hats the cheerful attendants wear tromping through the snow and operating the lifts at Grand Targhee.

In the New England towns and villages much of history never disappeared. Families still live in homes built two centuries ago. Tiny churches, which have been serving parishioners since the Revolution, or maybe the War of 1812, sit alongside computer stores. We've slept in graceful country inns that have been welcoming guests since the days they arrived by carriage—while across the highway are modern motels.

The East has neither an Aspen, with its sizzling atmosphere; nor a Vail, whose town is a cluster of elegant hotels interspersed with expensive shops; nor the luxury of Sun Valley, which introduced resort skiing to America.

But it does have Stowe, in northern Vermont, a charming and traditional New England village laced with enough prim white churches, bars, restaurants, shops, and motels to keep every visitor happy. And Lake Placid, in the famed Adirondacks, where American athletes train for every type of Winter Olympic sport.

Snow Quality

The ambience, the scenery, the shops, the housing, all are auxiliary to the bottom line—the skiing, and everything a resort does to make skiing itself the magnet that pulls us to it.

Let's talk snow talk.

No ski resorts in the United States, Canada, or Europe can boast lighter, fluffier snow than that which sprinkles down from the clouds over the high-elevation resorts of the West. However, except for off-trail skiing, or the first couple days after a storm, I've found virtually no difference between skiing a groomed slope at 8,000 feet in the West and one at 2,000 feet in the East. This is because after being pounded by skiers during the day, and smoothed out at night by the ponderous grooming machines that roar up and down the slopes of every major resort, the powder disappears. All the groomed trails are covered by packed snow, otherwise called packed powder. Period.

What *can* make a difference is the climate.

High-altitude resorts, with low humidity, tend to have a fairly stable winter climate: very cold at night but reaching into the 20s during the day. This climate preserves the smooth, skiable surfaces. And as a bonus, it's beautiful to sit outdoors after lunch to enhance your tan.

When it's cold in the East—and stays cold—the packed powder stays packed. However, eastern resorts bounce more frequently between the 30s during the day and the shivering teens and below at night. And because of their higher humidity, in eastern resorts subject to this temperature pattern the delicious texture of packed powder may become topped with an extrahard surface. Hey, I keep my edges sharp in Vermont.

To compensate for unreliable winter snows, the eastern resorts began to line their trails with snow guns in the 1970s. Today, almost every New England ski area boasts that 90 to 100 percent of its trails are covered by snowmaking.

All is not always perfect skiing in the West. To compensate for those winters when their slopes also are covered with more mud and crud than snow, western resorts quietly began installing snowmaking on their trails in the 1980s. Today they make it eminently clear that they, too, still offer skiing when nature forgets to roll in the winter clouds. Thank you, snowmakers.

Though modern snowmaking equipment produces a lighter and more powdery snow than the early guns did, there are still differences in texture between natural and man-made snow, east or west.

Vertical Drop

There continues to be a misconception that western resorts have unlimited vertical drops. The vertical has absolutely nothing to do with how steep the trails are. It's the difference in elevation between the summit and the base. Yes, the large resorts of the West are large. But the vertical drops of the great, open western resorts are far closer to those of the major eastern areas than is generally supposed.

Only one ski area in North America has a vertical higher than 5,000 feet—Whistler/Blackcomb, in Canada. Jackson Hole has a vertical of more than 4,000 feet. Less than a dozen areas in the United States have a vertical drop of more than 3,000 feet. Two are in the east—Killington and Whiteface.

Don't be confused by the fact that the base elevation of western resorts may be 7,000 to 8,000 feet, while it's 1,500 to 2,000 feet in New England. The average vertical, whether in the Rockies or the Appalachians, is around 2,500 feet.

When *Skiing* magazine searched out the "dirty dozen," the 12 longest and steepest regularly maintained trails in the nation reachable by ski lift, 5 were in the East, 7 in the West.

Eastern resorts have substantially widened and added to their trails in the past quarter century. Except for a few saved as souvenirs, long gone are the narrow, icy paths through trees that the heroic skiers of the 1930s and late '40s struggled to ski down.

Struggle is a mild word. I fought to navigate Roundabout, the narrow, never-groomed souvenir-of-yesterday trail at Killington. After bumping, turning, and twisting my way to the bottom I can only look with admiration upon anyone who managed to survive skiing it on wooden skis with metal edges wearing double leather boots locked into bear-trap bindings.

When *Powder* magazine fondly reviewed the few ancient New England trails that have managed to resist constant efforts to widen and groom them, it came up with an additional seven:

- Antelope and Fall Line Trails, Mad River Glen, Vermont;

- Robin's Run, Smuggler's Notch, Vermont;

- Wildcat Trail, Wildcat Mountain, New Hampshire;

- Goat, Stowe, Vermont;

- East Bowl, Burke, Vermont;

- Rumble, Sugarbush, Vermont.

Ski them before they disappear.

On the other hand, the dramatic powder bowls and wide-open slopes of the West will never disappear.

Three times America has played host to the Winter Olympics. Once at Squaw Valley, in the impressive Lake Tahoe region of California, and twice at Lake Placid and on the runs of nearby Whiteface. Squaw Valley has a vertical of 2,850 feet; Whiteface, 3,216 feet.

Utah will host the Winter Olympics in 2002. Congratulations. You gotta have it to host it.

SKIING THE GEMS

The snow was deep, the trails smoothly groomed, and the sun brilliant in a cloudless blue sky. It was an ideal winter day to be carving linked turns.

The mountain should have been crowded, the lift lines filled with impatient skiers. But the runs were packed with powder, not with skiers, and even the most impatient couldn't growl at a two-minute wait to board a swinging chair.

Where were the crowds?

They were having their fun and thrills skiing the great destination resorts. Those enjoying winter instead on these uncrowded trails were skiers who knew there also is pleasure in skiing any of the outstanding, low-key, alternative Gems of North America.

There are two major trade-offs for those who head for the gems rather than the crown jewels. The first can be summed up in one welcome word: *Prices!*

At the gems, everything from lift-ticket to ski school rates ranges from 10 to 50 percent below the rates at their destination neighbors.

The second is the pleasure of skiing in the relaxed atmosphere of a small resort that offers what you want in skiing, whether it be a family-oriented or a powder-country playground.

Most are close to cities. A few are hidden in distant mountains. While the average gem is small in terms of acreage and number of trails, a few are dramatically large. Usually they have perhaps three to six chairlifts—one or two which may have been upgraded to high-speed quads—and probably a couple surface lifts still dragging skiers uphill.

One gem may brag as loudly as a skier winning his or her first NAS-TAR gold if its lifts can tote as many as 3,000 skiers an hour to the summit. Another may be able to haul 8,000.

By comparison, destination areas have networks of lifts, including high-speed quads, often one or more gondolas, and cable cars with an hourly uphill capacity of 15,000 to more than 40,000 skiers. And they have crowds to match.

Value Skiing

Lift rates are a key to what it costs to ski a resort. In the mid-1990s a single adult weekend one-day lift ticket—the most expensive ticket at any area—ranged from $45 to $50 at the destination playgrounds. The national-average single adult weekend ticket at the gems was estimated at $28. Whooooeee.

There's an impression among some skiers that the gems are populated only by novices, families, and the girls' and boys' ski clubs from the local high school.

In reality, there's no way to classify the skiers who find their pleasure skiing the gems. They run the gamut: mogul-bashing pros; powder hounds; singles with a roving eye; easy-skiing seniors; families; kids; snowboarders; veterans of snowy mountain scenery; and newcomers to the glory of the sport, as well as the girls' and boys' ski clubs from the local high school.

There's as much variation among the gems as there is among those who ski them. Grand Targhee, high on the slopes of the soaring Tetons, has only three chairlifts on one of its two mountains. The other mountain is serviced by snowcat. But with the highest rate of natural snow of any ski area in the nation, it is a glorious place to ski powder, real, deep powder, or learn to.

Bretton Woods is three-quarters of a continent east, on the forested slopes of New Hampshire's White Mountains. Eighty percent of its 30 trails are green or blue. But within a casual drive of the slopes are charming villages and quaint inns dating back to the birth of the nation, and nearby is the magnificent Mount Washington Hotel, site of the historic Bretton Woods international financial conference in 1944.

Kelly Ladyga, communications director for 10 of the lesser resorts of Colorado that have banded together as "Gems of the Rockies," says: "While they may be smaller in size compared to other Colorado resorts, they are large in value, variety, and vertical!" Every year, "the demand for alternative skiing choices grows. In the 1994–95 season the Colorado gems hosted more than 1.2 million skier visits, growing more rapidly than any other segment of the ski area market." Novices are an important chunk of that market.

The gems have ski schools for kids and adults, nurseries, and day-care centers. They also have rental and repair shops on the premises. And even if they have only one cafeteria in a base lodge, you'll enjoy the taste of your hamburger and french fries more since you'll be paying about two-thirds the price that the same mouthful would cost at a destination jewel.

Gems also have snowmaking for those bleak times when there's only a smidgen of natural snow on the ground. They groom their runs, though perhaps not as frequently or vigorously as the big boys do.

The areas close to major population centers almost always have night skiing, a tremendous plus for the ski-hungry who can't zip away for an evening on the snow until the office closes at 5 o'clock.

The major disadvantage of gems for many skiers is size. Within a couple days, an aggressive skier may well have zipped down every slope. The challenge certainly is different at a destination giant, where it could take a week or more for an aggressive, nonstop expert to sample all the runs.

Sparkling après-ski facilities, an array of restaurants and busy on-site shopping centers, are not the specialty of the alternatives. A gem may have only a couple cheerful bars nearby to brighten the snowy country-side at night.

Housing is always limited close to the resort. Those tucked into out-of-the-way mountains usually have a hotel or two at the base; otherwise, look for motels, B&Bs, or a ski chalet or two in the neighborhood. Almost all have a housing bureau; or you can call the nearest chamber of commerce to locate facilities.

The off-slope activities found at, or near, many of the gems are the same as those found around the crown jewels: cross-country skiing, snowmobiling, snowshoeing, hayrides, saunas, heated pools, health spas, and sightseeing trips to local points of interest.

For those on a tight budget, or with only enough time for a quickie weekend holiday close to home, or who enjoy skiing in a relaxed atmosphere more than in the excitement of a crowd, the alternative gem may be precisely where you'll find what you want.

SKIING EUROPE

No matter what splendid ski resort he enjoys in the United States or Canada, a dream lurks in every true skier's soul of carving down the great slopes of Europe's Alps. And why not?

The scenery is spectacular. Skiing is generally above timberline on mountains of snow that extend from horizon to horizon. Most ski resorts have base-to-summit verticals that average 5,000 to 7,000 feet. Only a dozen in the United States are actually higher than 3,000 feet.

European ski areas range from large to enormous. Some are even larger. Consider, for example, the Val d'Isère-Tignes complex in France: 102 lifts, including T-bars, cable cars, gondolas, chairlifts, high-speed

Lech, Austria.

detachable quads, and an underground funicular, looking much like a New York City subway, which can whisk 3,000 skiers per hour from the base to the soaring glacier snows. The complex of lifts serves an impossible 200 square miles of skiing.

How about the Arlberg region of Austria? Five interconnected resorts—Lech, Zurs, St. Anton, St. Christoph, and Stuben—offer skiers 162 square miles of trails served by 86 lifts.

Nothing elsewhere in the world compares with the Trois Vallées in France—Val Thorens, Courchevel, Mirabel—with 200 lifts, 400 miles of marked runs, and an uphill capacity of 230,000 an hour.

Or ski with a guide from country to country, from Zermatt in Switzerland to Cervina in Italy, or from Courmayeur, on the Italian side of Mont Blanc, to Chamonix, on the French side, or between France and Switzerland.

Trails

European trails are marked green for gentle, red for intermediate, and black for the toughies. The green really means easy to low intermediate. However, the European concept of intermediate (red) runs includes those we'd mark as blacks. As for the actual blacks? They'd be double blacks at your favorite American ski area.

While there are always miles of green trails, most skiing is in the easy intermediate to low expert range. There are enough tough slopes, both on marked trails and "off piste," to challenge the most adventurous extreme skiers. For off-piste skiing it's wise to employ local licensed guides. Getting lost in a sudden mountain storm, or dropping into a glacial crevasse, is not conducive to either happy or healthy skiing.

The longest ski run in the world—actually on a face of the redoubtable Mont Blanc, the highest mountain in Europe—reachable by lifts is the Vallée Blanc at Chamonix. Two cable cars, in sequence, carry skiers to the summit of the Aguille du Midi, at about 13,000 feet.

I was with a group of three other skiers who arranged to hire a guide for this dynamic trip. In the guide office, a slender, friendly girl with a beautiful tan asked about our skiing skills: "Are you the good intermediates?"

We each assured her we were. That's when I discovered that when the French say a "good" intermediate, it's a polite way of referring to a skier who can handle low expert terrain.

Our Vallée Blanc experience was awesome. Getting off the cable car at the Aguille du Midi, we walked through a tunnel carved through the mountain's eternal glacial cap, strapped our skis on our backs, and roped up for a trip of a couple hundred yards down a narrow, icy incline to the snows. Then came every kind of skiing that a tremendous mountain can challenge you with. The steeps. Flats edging past vertical drops of several thousand feet and hundred-foot-deep icy crevasses. Wind-packed stretches of snow harder than ice. Slaloming through 6 inches of fresh powder.

Hours later we skied to an easy end to our trip at around 2,000 feet. The sun was shining, the birds were singing, the snow was dripping off the trees. I looked up at an impossible 11,000-foot vertical, grinned, and muttered, "Been there. Done that."

European skiing is generally on terrain of sloping glaciers heavily coated with winter snows high above the valley floor. The usual way to reach it is via a 60-to-150-passenger cable car—with skiers crunched shoulder to shoulder, holding onto their skis and wreathed with anticipation—then take chairlifts to the various trails on the snow-covered glaciers. The steepest pitches are usually on the tree-covered lower slopes below the glaciers, where the mountains plunge precipitously down to the valley floor.

Snowboarding

With open arms—well, with half-pipes and snowboard parks—the resorts of Europe welcome shredders. The sport has brought new excitement to the Alps as well as to the Rockies and the Appalachians. Snowboarding has not yet attracted the tens of thousands of younger people in Europe that it has in the United States, but their numbers are increasing swiftly. Snowboard parks are found throughout Alpine resorts.

One of the favorites in Europe among the snowboard crowd is Val Thorens, the newest and highest ski resort in the Alps. It's among the first to get the heavy snows of early winter, and the last to close in late spring. This is a tremendous attraction for snowboard maniacs, who'd rather ski breathtaking runs than enjoy the more sophisticated atmosphere of the older resorts.

When to Go

Generally, it's safest to head for the Alps after mid-January for late-winter and early-spring skiing when the snow is as dependable on the lower,

Tignes, France.

steep slopes as on the higher elevations. However, if you want to catch the magic of the Christmas season, go for the higher-altitude resorts. These include Lech, Zurs, and St. Christoph in the Arlberg; Courmayeur and Cervina in Italy; Tignes-Val d'Isère, Alpe d'Huez, and Val Thorens in France, and Zermatt and St. Moritz in Switzerland.

Several resorts offer glacier skiing throughout the summer. Summer skiing is chiefly on easy to intermediate runs. The cable cars carrying skiers to the snow fields start operating early in the morning and usually shut down around midafternoon, when the snow turns into mountain mush.

Oh, Those Lift Manners

Europeans find lift line manners a bore. Shoving and pushing are widely practiced, though not with the vigor of a few years ago. Some skiers will even say "pardon me" as they squeeze past. Don't let 'em.

Until around the mid-1980s, the casual attitude of the European resorts was that simply marking the treeless slopes with an occasional pole with a colored top indicating the degree of difficulty and the number of the trail, was all any skier really needed. So, ski them. Only a few trails were actually groomed.

On recent trips to the cluster of resorts at Chamonix in France, however, as well as the resorts of Italy and the magnificent Arlberg, we found a tremendous upgrading of trail maintenance. Miles of trails now are groomed, with growling snowcats roaring day and night. The one-time preponderance of T-bars and Pomas has largely been replaced with chairlifts, including high-speed detachable quads.

Housing

European ski areas are principally focused on a town whose older quarters have been around for hundreds of years but are now overwhelmed by modern hotels, condominiums, chalets, and shopping centers. In the Arlberg, even the newest hotels are architecturally harmonious with buildings 200 years old. In France, the newest are dramatic structures harmonious with the Alps.

Housing facilities have undergone a remarkable change over the years. On my first ski trip to France, in the 1970s, skiers stayed only in hotels or pleasant *pensions*, the European equivalent of a B&B. Today, modern condominium complexes are widely available. But be aware that

Chamonix, France.

when Europeans claim an apartment sleeps six, it will actually be comfortable for four.

Traditional hotels and *pensions,* small by American standards, are awarded up to five stars according to the number of amenities offered. As a rule of thumb, choose a facility of three stars or higher.

You'll normally get the best deal at a hotel if you accept it's breakfast-dinner meal plan. Generally, the manager will allow you to substitute lunch for dinner on the nights you want to dine out.

Ski Schools
The first ski school in the world opened in 1907 in Austria. The first trained ski instructors in the United States were Austrians hired by Sun Valley in 1936. Every European resort has ski schools for skiers of every age. While teaching techniques may differ, all schools group people by age and base skiing level. Little effort is made to offer specialized teaching for women by women instructors.

Children have their own facilities with their own specially qualified instructors. Ski school facilities for kids are, on the whole, less elaborate than those at American resorts. Children's instruction tends to be more structured, with less emphasis on "gee, this is fun" than you may be used to. But the kids really learn.

Child care is always available, though the usual minimum age is three.

Lift tickets are sold for a single day, a week, or longer; they're cheaper, of course, for lengthier stays. Many resorts offer discounts for children 12 and under, and free skiing for those 5 and under. Discounts, or free skiing, for seniors are the norm throughout Europe.

All resorts have ski rental shops. The quality of rental equipment is excellent. I recommend that you bring your own boots but rent skis and poles. If you don't have to haul your skis around—along with all the other gear you'll be loaded down with—you'll find yourself smiling knowingly at skiers struggling in and out of airports and taxis with theirs.

Food and Play

You expect and are rarely disappointed by the fine food available in European resort restaurants and hotels. However, what you may not expect is the superb quality of the food at mountain cafés, sometimes in remodeled ancient shepherd huts high above the valley. The luncheon meals and snacks we've enjoyed are a shocking reminder to Americans that there's more to lunch than pizza, cheeseburgers, hot dogs, and chicken salad. We've found ourselves overindulging in a *poulet au vin rouge*, or lentils Côte d'Azur, or a ragout of pork hocks, or bratwurst smothered in a hearty sauerkraut. Always the food must be accompanied by a stein of beer, or a bottle of wine, or a glass of schnapps.

The idea that skiers hit the slopes when the lift opens and, except for a quickie lunch, hurtle down the mountains all day is not quite the reality over there. Casual is the key. We've found ourselves joining those who enjoy a long lunch, then sitting outside for an hour or two, relaxed and suntanned faces staring blindly into the sun. Many Americans ski through midday lunch period because Europeans tend to be punctual about stowing their skis when it's time for a gourmet snack and the slopes are almost empty; the Americans don't then indulge in food until after about 1 P.M. Europeans often stop for an afternoon drink, sometimes in a mountain restaurant or a ski-in, ski-out bar, then don't indulge again until at least after their final run, when they relax with an aperitif before heading to their hotel, chalet, or condo. All part of the pleasure of skiing the Alps.

Après Fun

Europeans can ski as hard by day and drink as much by night as Americans. There's less noise after dark in some countries, while in others all-night partying competes with sunlight skiing.

Switzerland is known more for moderation than wild partying. The little areas are quiet. It's in the bigger resorts that the discos and bars are alive, noisy, and smoke filled until about midnight.

Austrians are exuberant party skiers during the day as well as at night in the large resorts. Roistering begins before the lifts close, slows down during the dinner hour, then erupts again with disco parties that don't really start until 11 P.M.

The ebullient nightlife in the French resorts also doesn't being to swing until around 11 P.M. Serious players hang in until 3 or 4 in the morning.

Italians are late-night carousers, but spend the time doing as much talking and ardent debating as dancing.

Travel

Individual travel to European resorts is more complex than heading for a ski holiday in Vermont or Colorado. First there's the usual problem of time—leaving the East Coast in the evening and arriving in Europe when your body thinks it should be the middle of the night. Then there's getting from the airport to the ski area. This can involve renting a car—make sure your rented car has chains as well as a ski rack if you're bringing your own skis—or taking a train or bus. If you're arranging your own travel schedule, allow for the type and time of transportation.

An American driver's license is generally acceptable throughout Europe if you're 21 or older and the license has been in effect for at least a year. The international license issued by the AAA is not necessary, but it's good to have as an alternative.

Unless you're willing to take the time and effort required to search out the best ski holiday bargains on your own, check ski clubs and charter groups. Not only will a group trip likely be the least-expensive way to enjoy your holiday in the Alps, but it will also take care of all the problems of flying, getting to the resort, and housing efficiently.

The best rates for housing and at many restaurants are during low season, when they may run 15 to 20 percent less than during high season. Low season normally runs from December 1 to the weekend before Christmas, then from the weekend after New Year's through early February, and finally from the end of March to the end of skiing.

Insurance

Whether you're traveling via regular commercial flight, on a charter airline, or with an organized tour, it's advisable to have trip-cancellation insurance in case something goes wrong. The cost to you otherwise could be the total price of the trip—on which you didn't go.

European resorts are casual about hazards and ski boundaries, which aren't always well marked. Skiers are more responsible for their own safety than in this country. If something goes wrong rescue operations are expensive—and the skier pays. If you're skiing France, a Carte Neige insurance policy for around $35 will pay all rescue and medical costs for a full season.

Don't even think of touching a car until you've verified that you're fully covered by insurance, either through your own automobile policy, your credit card, or insurance offered by the car rental company.

Weather

Naturally, go dressed for winter. However, Alpine winters are generally mild, with daytime temperatures in the lower 20s.

Alpine snow is slightly heavier than the snow at the resorts in the higher elevations of the Rockies, but drier than that in the low altitudes of New England.

Only a couple resorts in all Europe are actually above the 7,000-foot level. What this means to the average skier flying in from a low elevation is that the unspoken problem of altitude sickness remains unspoken, because it's virtually nonexistent.

Money

Paying by traveler's check or credit card is no longer a hassle in Europe. The most widely accepted credit cards are Visa, American Express, MasterCard (called Eurocard in Europe), Diners Club, and Carte Blanche.

ATMs are widely available and will give you money in local currency. Check with your own credit card company or bank, however, on whether its card is usable in the country in which you'll be challenging those broad, above-treeline slopes.

If you exchange American money or traveler's checks for local currency, you'll always find the best rate in banks, the worst rate at your hotel, and the next worst at currency exchange offices, including the one staring at you as you walk through the airport looking for a taxi.

Whenever possible, use a credit card for all transactions. This applies to lift tickets as well as all other purchases. Only a few resorts accept them, though. You'll be charged at the most advantageous exchange rate when your bill stares you in the face as you sit at home reminiscing over the pleasure and excitement of your recent trip.

Safeguards

The usual safeguards for smart travelers are especially important when in a foreign country. Make copies of your passport and other important documents. Keep a list handy of your credit cards. They do get stolen. If you doubt that, ask us. My wife's wallet, with credit cards and some American cash, disappeared from inside a should bag she was wearing during a five-minute stop in a theater ticket shop while we inquired about attending a ballet. Who picks ballet lovers' pockets?

Shopping

If you're looking for anything in the way of ski gear or clothing, compare the prices in Europe with those at home. Many brands of skis, boots, and bindings are made in Europe and less expensive there than in American shops.

Information

European tourist offices can provide you with general information, as well as specific information about individual resorts. Contact them at:

Austrian tourist offices: 500 Fifth Avenue, New York, NY 10110, (212) 944-6880; 500 North Michigan Avenue, Chicago, IL 60611, (312) 644-5556; 11601 Wilshire Boulevard, Los Angeles, CA 90025, (213) 477-3332; 2 Bloor Street East, No. 3330, Toronto CANADA, (416) 967-3381.

French tourist offices: 610 Fifth Avenue, New York, NY 10020, (212) 757-1125; 645 North Michigan Avenue, Chicago, IL 60611, (312) 337-6301; 9401 Wilshire Boulevard, Beverly Hills, CA 90212, (213) 271-6665; 1 Dundas Street, West, Toronto M4W 1A8, CANADA, (416) 593-4717.

German tourist offices: 122 East 42nd Street, New York, NY 10168, (212) 661-7200; 1176 Wilshire Boulevard, Los Angeles, CA 90025, (310) 575-9799.

Italian tourist offices: 630 Fifth Avenue, New York, NY 10111, (212) 245-4822; 500 North Michigan Avenue, Chicago, IL 60611, (312) 644-0990; 12400 Wilshire Boulevard, Suite 550, Los Angeles, CA 90025, (310) 820-0098; Place Ville Marie, Montreal, CANADA, (514) 868-7667.

Swiss tourist offices: 608 Fifth Avenue, New York, NY 10020, (212) 757-5944; 150 North Michigan Avenue, Chicago, IL 60601, (312) 630-5840; 260 Stockton Street, San Francisco, CA 94108, (415) 362-2260; 222 North Sepulveda Boulevard, El Segunda, CA 90245, (310) 335-5980; 926 East Mall, Etobicoke, Ontario M9B 6K1, CANADA, (416) 971-6425.

Another excellent source of information on skiing Europe are European airlines. Air France, Swissair, Lufthansa, KLM, and Finnair usually offer special ski packages every winter. Ski packages to Europe and South America are offered by a number of commercial tour operators. Unless you know the tour operator, however, it's wise to check on its reputation before signing up. And, naturally, many travel agencies offer European ski packages. The agencies generally have a better reputation for providing precisely what they advertise than do some of the commercial tours.

THE SKIER'S DOZEN

What sets a ski resort apart from its neighbors? Its size? Number of lifts? Scenery? History? Location? Annual snowfall in feet? Vertical? Après-ski fun? Snowmaking? Unique background? Elegance?

Answer: Any or all of the above.

To name the 50 or 100 greatest ski resorts in the nation, or in Europe, or the best in the West, or New England, is quite a simple task. Pick out the largest and, voilà! There they are.

I've long pondered a question once asked of me about the places I've skied. It was not the usual, "Which is your favorite?" For that I have a stock—and true—answer: The one I'm skiing at the moment. The question was: "What are the dozen outstanding resorts in the nation?"

The dozen? I could name, easily, the 50 or the 100. But to whittle that number down to 12? And, besides, what would make any of the 12 "outstanding"?

Suffice it to say that after consideration I did, in time, come up with a "skier's dozen"—13 resorts, ranging from a tiny gem that's swathed in deep powder every winter to one of the most elegant destination resorts in the world.

They all have only one thing in common—each is a tad different from any other resort. It has a tremendous size or location, or a unique role in skiing history. It's not a "better place" to ski than dozens of others.

Following is a brief visit to each of them:

A-Basin

Officially, the name is Arapahoe Basin. But its friends simply call it "A-Basin." It's the kind of place you brag about skiing, not, of course, in loud and vulgar tones, but softly, so those who know it instantly understand where you had the courage, and the skill, to enjoy high-altitude snow.

High altitude? A-Basin begins higher than where almost every other soaring western ski resort leaves off. The base elevation is 10,780 feet. Once you're acclimated to this altitude be grateful that the vertical is only 1,670 feet. Which, of course, means that when you edge off the Lenawee lift you're at the 12,450-foot level, the highest point served by a ski lift in North America. Having caught your breath, look up, and you may see a few hearty souls climbing to the 13,050-foot summit of A-Basin on the spine of the Continental Divide to hurtle down never-groomed double-black-diamond cliffs to where trails begin.

Not to fret. There are enough double-black chutes, bowls, powder fields, and glades reachable by lifts to challenge the expert you think you are. Don't lose your nerve. It's embarrassing to take off your skis and hike down to the few easier trails. There are some. In fact, a generous 10 percent of A-Basin's terrain is for beginners. Only a modest 40 percent of the marked trails is for the dedicated demons of the dazzling descent. The rest of the area's 490 acres can actually be handled by competent intermediates.

We found it helpful when, on our first visit to this spectacular area— only a five-minute shuttle ride from Keystone, a destination resort where

A-Basin.

we were enjoying a ski holiday—new skiers were invited on a guided tour of the mountain. Before we began, however, the tour organizer didn't ask how good we were.

He pointed to one guide waving to us at the bottom of a black-diamond chute, and a second waiting on an intermediate trail.

"Ski to one of them for your tour," he called out. "That's the kind of terrain you'll ski. Go for it."

When you want to give your legs and lungs a rest, while frolicking on the slopes of A-Basin, relax and enjoy the fantastic view. The soaring, rugged peaks are riveting.

Aspen

Onmia Aspeni divisa in partes tres est.

First, it's heart is a small western town tucked into the Rockies. Second, to the world it's a land of chic and sex, glamour and fashion,

Aspen

gourmet restaurants and endless nightlife. Third, the skiing is damn good—for those who actually fly there to ski.

Indeed, skiing often seems a sideline in this old cowboy and rancher town that has become a playground for today's and tomorrow's stars from New York and Hollywood, where the nouveau riche are as enthusiastically welcomed to the land of glitz and glitter as is anyone else with money. And where gala festivals devoted to food and wine, comedy and the arts, stumble over each other.

There are also moderate restaurants and shops and casual nightspots for the skiers who have to keep careful account of the bucks that go into their ski holidays.

The glamorous life is centered in the town itself, and so is the skiing. Stores and shops edge right up to the four double chairlifts, three quads, and one gondola that whisk skiers up the challenging slopes of the area's major ski center, Aspen Mountain, with a vertical of 3,260 feet.

The mountain, known to locals as Ajax, is no place for beginners and nervous low intermediates. All the trails are for intermediates to experts, and for them it's a dynamite place to enjoy their skiing skills.

Two other local mountains have more than enough skiing for everyone from never-evers to double-black-diamond skiers. Tiehack/Buttermilk, with a vertical of 2,030 feet, is lined with easy green to high intermediate runs. Aspen Highlands has the highest vertical in Colorado—3,800 feet—and could be described as a "well-balanced" mountain with a full range of runs for all levels of skiers.

There's snowmaking on all three mountains for those times when, even in Colorado, nature is penurious with natural snows.

Both Aspen Highlands and Tiehack/Buttermilk are open to shredders, but Aspen Mountain is off-limits to the snowboard crowd.

Cross-country addicts have 80 km of free groomed trails, the most extensive network of free runs in America, courtesy of Aspen's Nordic Council.

If indulging a passion for off-slope mountain skiing is on your agenda, one trail system with huts for overnight stops links Aspen with the Crested Butte ski resort, and another trail with huts, named after the famed 10th Mountain division that trained for combat near here in World War II, links Aspen with Vail. As a footnote to the division's history, Senator Robert A. Dole lost the use of his right hand as a combat lieutenant with the 10th when he was injured while leading an attack against German lines in World War II.

In addition to luxury housing, motels and modest condominiums are widely available.

All three of the mountains offer free tickets to seniors 70-plus, and to children under 6.

For information, call the Aspen Chamber Resort Association at (800) 262-7736. On the Internet: http://s2.com/skiaspen.

Bretton Woods

Edging off Fabayan's Express triple chair at the 3,100-foot summit of Bretton Woods, skiers can take a moment to enjoy the imposing view across the Ammonoosuc Valley to 6,200-foot Mount Washington, the highest peak in the northeast. There's one significant difference between the summits of Mount Washington and Bretton Woods: wind.

Sweeping in from Canada, winds have buffeted Mount Washington with the highest velocity ever recorded in the world—more than 220 miles per hour. As for Bretton Woods, since the resort opened in 1973,

Bretton Woods.

the summit lift has been closed for only two hours on one day because of wind gusts.

Skiers also can look down into the valley at international history—the magnificent Mount Washington Hotel. There, in 1944, while the world still was embroiled in war, delegates from the Allied powers met in this quiet corner of bucolic New England to organize the International Bank for Reconstruction and Development. The meeting still is known as the Bretton Woods Conference.

Indeed, with the exception of the construction of the ski resort, the area has changed little in the past century. Charming inns still greet customers who once rode up in horse and buggy. Visitors are genuinely welcomed at church dinners serving the same traditional New England foods that were heaped high on plates at church dinners 150 years ago.

Tiny villages, whose roots go back to the 1700s, and whose antiques shops sell mementos of those years, are scattered along highways where motorists actually observe BRAKE FOR MOOSE warnings.

Skiing is centered on a single mountain with 30 trails. Thirty percent are green, 45 percent intermediate, and 25 percent black diamond. Snowboarders can play on a 400-foot accelerator half-pipe. There's a 90-km network of marked and groomed Nordic trails. The Nordic ski center is in the Mount Washington Hotel.

Snowmaking covers 98 percent of the slopes, which are served by two double chairs, one triple, one detachable quad, and one surface lift. There's night skiing every Friday and Saturday.

At the ski area's base are the usual shops and restaurants, ski schools, and facilities for babies and youngsters.

Bretton Woods offers the most unusual activity at any ski resort in the nation: novice races and clinics for rifle ski biathlons and archery ski biathlons.

There are only six lodging facilities, ranging from motels to slope-side town houses, close to the base. Additional housing is in nearby towns.

Swinging après-ski life is not one of the major attractions in this quiet corner of New Hampshire. Antiquing is. You'll need your own car to cruise the antiques shops scattered throughout the countryside of this corner of historic America.

For information: Bretton Woods Ski Resort, Bretton Woods, NH 03575; (800) 232-2972; Housing hotline: (800) 258-0330. The Twin Mountain Chamber of Commerce has information on area housing: (800) 245-8946. On the Internet: www.brettonwoods.com. E-mail: skibw@brettonwoods.com.

Grand Targhee

What do you do when 1,500 pounds of Moose ambles casually out from the trees and stops dead below you in the middle of a powder ski run?

Nothing. Absolutely nothing.

You wait until that big hulk of a creature decides to mosey on. Sighting game—moose, elk, deer, coyotes, high-leaping jackrabbits escaping hungry mountain lions while bald eagles soar overhead—is only one of the unusual attractions at this dynamic gem on the western slopes of the majestic Grand Tetons in the northwestern corner of Wyoming, close to Yellowstone National Park.

Another is the awesome fact that it averages 500 inches, or more than 40 feet, of snow every winter. The snows are so dependable that Grand Targhee's envied slogan is: "Snow from heaven, not hoses."

All skiing is on two adjacent peaks: Peaked Peak and Fred's Peak.

Peaked Peak, with a 2,800-foot vertical, is never groomed. It's a powder paradise and its long fall-line slopes are perfectly suited to learn powder skiing. It can be reached by snowcat. Tickets include a guide,

Grand Targhee.

powder lessons, and a small transmitter to slip into your pocket so you can be located if you have to be dug out of a snow slide.

Fred's Peak, with a 2,200-foot vertical, is served by three chairlifts and a surface lift. Groomed trails cover only a quarter of the mountain. The rest is left untouched for the glorious benefit of powder, or would-be powder, skiers. Seventy percent of the skiing is rated intermediate on both mountains; 20 percent is in the expert to extreme range; and only 10 percent is for novices and beginners.

Snowboarders are as welcome as skiers both on the snowcat trips and on Fred's, with its permanent snowboard half-pipe to play on.

There are 15 km of maintained cross-country ski trails that range from flat and easy to most difficult.

Nordic skiers have a wide range of breathtaking backcountry options. Guided tours, on either skis or snowmobiles, range across the nearby woods and into the high country with views of Greater Yellowstone.

It's important to note that the resort suffered a major disaster in March 1990 when fire swept through the base area. Quickly rebuilt, the new base area, a cluster of lodgepole and stucco buildings with a southwestern flavor, won a top design award a year later from *Snow Country* magazine. The base includes the usual stores, restaurants, condos, hotels, and one bar. Readers also voted Grand Targhee one of the top five resorts in North America for snowfall, scenery, snow surface, accuracy of snow reports, food, and service.

You'll never find a more amiable bunch of folks serving you than the local ranchers and cowboys who, for years, have stabled their horses and spent winters taking care of skiers here. I've always felt their 10-gallon hats just go naturally with the relaxed, friendly western spirit that pervades this gem.

There are only some 1,200 beds in the area. Many skiers rent condos in Jackson, 38 miles away.

Facilities for kids range from a nursery for infants to special mountain and powder classes for teenagers. The 12-and-under ski free, one child with each paying adult.

Grand Targhee is 290 miles north of Salt Lake City; 137 miles northeast of the author's hometown, Pocatello; 87 miles from Idaho Falls; and 42 miles from Jackson. Resort shuttle service is available at airports in Idaho Falls and Jackson, children free. Reservations are required. An express bus runs daily between Jackson and Grand Targhee. The fee includes a lift ticket.

One advisory: The base elevation is 8,000 feet. Skiers not used to high altitudes should take it easy for the first couple days. For all queries, from housing to snow reports, call (800) TARGHEE (827-4433).

Hunter Mountain

Hunter Mountain is, quite simply, the busiest weekend-only destination ski resort in the nation.

And, quite simply, destination resorts are where skiers go for one- and two-week holidays, not for a weekend vacation, leaving the slopes all but deserted Monday through Friday.

But then Hunter is special. It's where the subway crowd from the Bronx and Brooklyn and Queens and Staten Island and, oh yes, even Manhattan party and ski and snowboard when time is short. Dynamite slopes always covered with snow—man-made or natural—are only a couple hours away in Rip Van Winkle's Catskills.

The ski complex is comprised of four separate areas: (1) Hunter One, a beginner's area; (2) Hunter Mountain, basically for those intermediate to expert; (3) Hunter West, strictly for the hotshot black-diamond crowd; and (4) the local villages—ah, but more about them in a moment. As far as the subway tribe is concerned, anyone with a ski ticket can ski anything. At any given moment, 50 percent of those who are skiing, skidding, racing, and tumbling down Hunter Mountain's intermediate slopes range from beginners to advanced beginners.

However, only true double-black-diamond fiends even stare down the dizzying cliff called K27. *Skiing* magazine included it in a list of the 12 meanest, steepest ski runs in the nation serviced by a lift.

Orville and Izzy Slutzky, the owners of Hunter, defied all the odds when they acquired the area 35 years ago. Experts predicted no ski resort could survive the rocky terrain and mixed winter weather conditions in the Catskills.

But the Slutzkys began experimenting with snowmaking, then in its infancy. Hunter became the first ski area in the world to pour enough man-made snow to cover every one of its 49 trails, served by 15 lifts from base to summit. It still prides itself as "The Snow Making Capital of the World."

Hunter Mountain.

The large and crowded base lodge includes two cafeterias, a sushi parlor, an undulating bar crowded four-deep all day with thirsty skiers, a deli, a pizza shop, a gourmet restaurant, an art gallery featuring the paintings, photographs and handicrafts of local artists, a ski museum, as ski shop, rentals, a repair shop, a first-aid center, and a nursery-play area. At the summit there's a bleak, silo-shaped stone lodge to slip inside only if it's necessary to warm up on a cold day.

When the lifts fall silent on the weekends, the crowds flood through the nearby villages of Hunter, Tannersville, and Haines Falls for some of the liveliest, noisiest après-ski fun in the country. The entire country. Go to sleep, Aspen.

The villages also have every variety of lodging, from B&Bs to elegant resort hotels, and cafés that range from pizza parlors to three-star eateries.

For information: Hunter Mountain, P.O. Box 295, Hunter, NY 12442, (518) 263-4223; housing: (800) 775-4641; snow: (800) 367-7669. E-mail: hunter@albanyny.net. On the Internet: http://www.huntermtn.com.

Killington

Terrain, snow, grooming, dining, après-ski life, and great skiing were all cited by *Skiing* magazine when it included Killington in its "top 15" destination ski resorts internationally. The magazine was accurate on every point.

Killington is the largest resort in New England. Its 75 miles of trails spread across six mountains cover 1,000 acres. With a vertical drop of 3,150 feet, it's one of only a dozen ski area in the nation with a vertical of more than 3,000 feet. The summit, Killington Peak, has an elevation of 4,220 feet. Legend has it that an early minister gazing across the endless forests from the mountain named the country Vermont, meaning "Green Mountains" in French.

One of the fast-moving pioneers in snowmaking, Killington covers 44 miles of trails with man-made snow, turning on the guns at the first hint of winter frost and shutting them down only when they spray water. Its fleet of 21 state-of-the-art snowcats is not only one of the largest in the nation but probably spends more time grooming the slopes than any two other areas combined.

Killington has five double chairlifts, four triples, seven quads— including two detachables—and two surface lifts with a combined capacity of more than 35,000 skiers an hour.

The pièce de résistance is the Skyeship, a gondola with eight-passenger cabins, each individually decorated and heated and featuring piped-in music. It's the longest lift in the United States, covering 2.5 miles from its base station to Skye Peak.

Skiing is largely on modest to high intermediate terrain, but with enough black-diamond runs, especially on Bear Mountain, to win *Ski* magazine's designation as the Number One spot in the East to challenge double-black-diamond steeps.

One of Killington's great attractions for the never-ever crowd is Snowshed, a ¾-mile-long and -wide beginner area as flat as a tilted pool table. The resort also boasts the longest single ski trail in the nation, Juggernaut, an easy cruising run for alpine and cross-country skiers that drops 3,100 feet on its 10-mile trip to the bottom.

Shredders are welcome. The resort has created a snowboard park with a half-pipe specifically for snowboarders.

Forty km of groomed cross-country trails are covered with snow-making.

Killington.

Killington skiers are served by five different base lodges—each with ski shops and rental facilities—seven cafeterias, one gourmet restaurant, and one mountaintop café.

The Children's Center has day-care programs for infants as young as six weeks and kids of up to six years. Ski classes are offered for kids from 3 to 12. Adult programs include special classes for women, taught by women, in both skiing and snowboarding.

Killington is not anchored to a base village. There are hotels, chalets, and condos at Killington and scattered throughout the area. The 5-mile access road that links Killington to U. S. Routes 4 and 100 is loaded with shops, bars, and restaurants. Here's where the après-ski life explodes when the lifts stop.

For information, write for a Killington Ski Week Guide, 403 Killington Road, Killington, VT 05751; (800) 372-2007. For e-mail: info@killington.com. On the Internet: www.killington.com.

Lake Placid

If there's an international winter sports center, its name is Lake Placid.

Not only does it hold the distinction of having hosted two Winter Olympic meets, in 1932 and again in 1980, but more than 8,000 world-class athletes annually train and compete here in every conceivable winter sport.

Now, hold your breath: Visitors are welcome to use any of the training facilities, whether it's zigging and zagging on a bobsled at a screaming 50 miles an hour down the lower half of the Olympic bobsled track—with a professional driver and brakeman on the sled with you—or gulping when you get off a glass elevator that carries sightseers 26 stories to the top of the 90-meter ski jump ramp. Fortunately, your ticket is good for a round trip.

Competing with the bobsled at providing terrifying thrills to courageous visitors is the Olympic luge.

Nearby is the Whiteface Mountain Ski complex with its vertical of 3,216 feet—the highest in the East. If you're an advanced intermediate looking for a precipitous thrill, challenge the expert men's and women's downhill 1980 Olympic runs from the summit, where the view of the Adirondack wilderness, the 6-million-acre New York State park, is spectacular.

Lake Placid.

Whiteface offers more runs for experts and beginners than intermediates on the main mountain, but adjacent Little Whiteface is laced with intermediate trails. The ski resort has all the usual facilities—ski schools, rentals, and a special children's center, though the latter doesn't accept youngsters less than two years old.

After a day on the mountain, try your own skating skills on the Olympic Oval rink at night.

Want more?

Cross-country skiers have access to the 50-km complex of groomed 15-foot-wide trails, which includes 10 marked runs: 3 novice, 6 intermediate, and 1 expert. Be careful. You might find an international champion practicing on your slope.

For those who wish to take a break from the more ardent activities, there always seems to be a local, national, or international competition in some winter event, from ski biathlon to ski jumping and snowboarding.

If watching is not on your itinerary, enjoy an afternoon dogsledding, or take the family for a nighttime toboggan run. You can pile up to six kids on a toboggan and ride a lighted ramp that ends with a roaring swoosh across the star-studded darkness of Mirror Lake.

Lake Placid itself is a remarkably beautiful community whose charm is reminiscent of that of old European ski towns. Among the usual shops is a noted art center that features the artistic and handicraft skills of Adirondack artisans. Whiteface Mountain, for downhill skiing, and Mount Hovenberg, for cross-country skiing and the luge and bob runs, are each about 8 miles from the center of the town, which is dominated by the huge Olympic center with its indoor hockey rink and outdoor staking rink. Buses run regularly between them, but it's nice to have a car.

For information: Lake Placid Visitors Bureau, Lake Placid, NY 12946; (518) 523-2445. Or Olympic Regional Development Authority, Lake Placid, NY 12946; (800) 462-6236. On the Internet: www.orda.org.

Snowshoe

Snowshoe is different, but only in a couple ways.

For example: The resort sits atop a U-shaped basin at the summit of Cheat Mountain, not at the base, as all properly designed ski areas are supposed to.

Snowshoe Mountain Resort.

And the altitude of the mountain is 4,840 feet, higher than any ski area in New England.

But then Snowshoe isn't in New England. It's south of the Mason-Dixon Line in West (by God) Virginia, which explains why it's probably far better known to Civil War buffs than to most skiers around the nation.

On the other hand, whether they're aficionados of old battlegrounds or old ski resorts, those who take to the slopes at Snowshoe will discover that skiing in the Old South can be an unexpectedly pleasant and challenging experience.

From the summit down to the base of the 11 chairlifts, the resort has a very respectable vertical of 1,500 feet and is laced with 53 trails, including a few tough enough to challenge black-diamond hotshots. For the most part, the well-maintained runs range from green to advanced blue.

The phrase "southern skiing" may sound like an oxymoron in a land of sunshine and cotton, but there are a few resorts scattered across the region and, among them, Snowshoe is the snowiest. It has an average annual snowfall of almost 200 inches, and today covers 95 percent of its slopes with high-tech snowmaking. Its season normally runs from mid-November to as far into April as the snows last.

Although it has no special snowboard facilities, snowboarders are welcome. Maybe due to southern manners, they have a deserved reputation for being more polite and less grungy here than they are elsewhere. I should also note that there's less shoving and more chivalry on the lift lines than at any resort I've ever skied.

Pleasantly remote from everywhere else—it's 26 miles to the nearest small town, Marlinton—Snowshoe Village, at the top of the mountain, is a collection of lodges, condominiums, chalets, shops, restaurants, and bars.

Gourmet southern mountain cuisine and local wild game are the famed specialties of The Red Fox Restaurant. The Comedy Cellar, the loudest bar on the mountain, features the ski world's only full-time resident comedian. When he's not pelting après skiers with humor, he cavorts during the day as the resort's mascot, Snowshoe Hare.

Kids squeal with delight when they spot actual snowshoe rabbits bouncing across the runs.

There's a full range of rentals, a ski shop, adult ski classes, and children's facilities, including an excellent day-care center and the Brr Rabbit ski school.

For information, including advice on mountain road conditions, call the resort at (304) 572-1000, or write: Snowshoe Resort, Snowshoe, WV 26209. On the Internet: wvweb.com/www/snowshoe.html.

Squaw Valley

Twice the Lake Tahoe region has garnered international attention.

The first occasion was in 1846, when a party of California-bound covered-wagon travelers found themselves trapped for the winter by tremendous snows north of Lake Tahoe. An unusual diet enabled many to survive. Of course you've heard of them. The Donner Party.

The second was in 1960, when Squaw Valley, a ski area west of Lake Tahoe, had already become a winter playground because of its tremendous snows. Of course you've heard what happened. It was the Winter Olympics. They were held in the United States that year for the second time.

The event, widely covered by television, a medium then comparatively new to winter sports, helped spark a national boom in skiing. In the Lake Tahoe region, new ski areas popped up faster than daffodils in spring.

For years, Squaw Valley was content to let the publicity laurels it garnered from its Olympic winter attract skiers to its fabulous terrain, basically monstrous, wide-open bowls with usually plentiful snows. The Lake Tahoe region, when viewed from the tops of Squaw Valley lifts, is one of the dramatic mountain areas in the world.

Then suddenly, a few years ago, Squaw Valley began a major effort to move into the class of world resorts.

It expanded its long-inadequate lift capacity to serve the 4,200 acres of skiable terrain and built more hotels, condominiums, shops, gourmet restaurants, bars, and amenities. However, despite this welcome expansion, the leaping après-ski nightlife is in nearby Truckee, on the California side, and Reno, across the border in Nevada.

Approximately 25 percent of the trails at the six peaks that make up the ski complex are for those who seek the wild challenge of extreme mountain skiing, or double black diamonds. The rest of the bowls and the few carved runs are about 50 percent for intermediate skiers, and 25 percent for beginners and never-evers.

Snowboarders are welcome and enjoy a special park and the inevitable snow pipe in an area reserved for shredders.

Squaw Valley.

Three hundred km of cross-country trails can be skied from Squaw Valley throughout the Lake Tahoe district.

As with all the resorts in the area, one other reason for Squaw Valley's popularity—let's face it—is Nevada's roaring, never-silent, always-beckoning next-door gambling casinos. To ensure that skiers who'd rather gamble than frolic on the mountains can get to them quickly, free buses run regularly between the snowy slopes and the clattering slot machines begging for nourishment from tourist bucks.

Squaw Valley's skiers are served by a 125-person cable car, a 6-passenger gondola, and 24 chairlifts, ranging from doubles to high-speed detachable quads.

The area's base elevation is 6,200 feet, which means that skiers rarely have any problem with the altitude. The vertical is 2,850 feet.

For general information at Squaw Valley, write Squaw Valley USA, Squaw Valley, CA 96146; (916) 583-6985; reservations: (800) 545-4350. On e-mail: squaw@squaw. On the Internet: http://www.squaw.com.

Stowe

The Oliver Luce family, the first settlers in what is now Stowe in northern Vermont, trimmed trees to build their home in 1794. Within a few years the Luces had opened an inn and a tavern to provide bed, board, and copious drinks to travelers.

In the 1930s, skiers, locked onto wooden skis with bear-trap bindings, discovered the joy of hanging onto rope tows that dragged them up the slopes of nearby Mount Mansfield so they could fight their way down a couple narrow, twisting trails through the thick woods. They arrived by the overnight ski train special, and they played and slept at local inns that provided them with bed, board, and copious drinks.

When the Von Trapp family fled Austria and brought *The Sound of Music* to Vermont, they opened a lodge here in 1940, the same year that Stowe replaced one rope tow with a small chairlift to the summit of Mount Mansfield—at 4,393 feet, the highest in Vermont.

After World War II, Stowe was the first area in the East to develop into a true destination ski resort. More lifts and trails were added to the mountain. The parents of the baby-boomer generation found all they wanted in terms of amenities at the new inns and lodges that opened in Stowe itself and along the access road to Mansfield. But then, for some inexplicable reason, in the early 1980s Stowe stopped expanding and improving and rested on its enviable reputation.

Meanwhile, many of the region's little playgrounds of rope tows and narrow trails blossomed into major ski areas with more and better housing facilities, and skiing, and services than Stowe.

All that has changed. Stowe today is vibrant with a new life that came from pumping the millions of dollars it found necessary to climb back into the ranks of the first-class ski resorts of America.

By way of example, long after its neighbors had begun covering their slopes with snowmaking, Stowe finally got around to installing a comprehensive snowmaking system. Now, 75 percent of the ski terrain on the two mountains, Mansfield and adjacent Spruce Peak, can be blanketed with white when winter is miserly. They're served by 10 lifts, including high-speed detachable quads, plus a gondola. Skiers can frolic or challenge themselves on 39 miles of wide, groomed trails.

So impressive is Stowe today that it was ranked Number One by *Ski* magazine's readers in a 1996 survey of New England ski areas.

Stowe.

Of course, some things haven't changed. The double-black hotshots can still attempt the fabled "Front Four" trails—Goat, Starr, National, and Liftline—that have been a trademark of the resort almost from its founding days. For the rest of us, some 75 percent of the runs are for novice to strong intermediate skiers.

Snowboarders are welcome. Spruce Peak has one of the largest half-pipes for shredders in all New England.

Four touring areas provide more than 150 km of groomed and tracked trails for cross-country enthusiasts.

Stowe itself is essentially a small town, with its famous white-steepled Community Church towering over the other buildings. The town was designated a National Historic District in 1978. Its numerous shops and cafés and, more than anything else, ambience of old New England make it a delightful place to walk around.

But most restaurants, hotels, motels, and après-ski pubs are strung along the 7-mile access road that stretches from Stowe to the mountain. Barhopping means hopping in your car.

The most famous place to stay is the Trapp Family Lodge, which is almost a self-contained cross-country ski resort in its own right. The Mount Mansfield Resort is a complex of condominiums and a hotel at the base of the mountain.

For information call the Stowe Area Association at (800) 24-STOWE. Or: Stowe Mountain Resort, 5781 Mountain Road, Stowe, VT 05672; (802) 253-3000; for reservations at the resort only: (800) 253-4754. On the Internet: www.stoweinfo.com.

Sun Valley

Sitting inside the grand palace that is the elegant Sun Valley Lodge, you can look across bathers in an outdoor heated circular pool—the first ever built by a ski resort—to towering Old Baldy, a majestic mountain laced with wide ski trails down its 3,400-foot vertical, one of the biggest in the nation.

Or you can glance in the other direction and see the huge ice skating rink where, in 1941, Sonja Henie, queen of the ice, starred in an unforgettable film classic, *Sun Valley Serenade*. The movie is still shown nightly in the Sun Valley Village theater, along with major current films.

Opened in 1936, the first destination ski resort in the nation, Sun Valley has never lost its preeminence as a winter playground.

Sun Valley.

Mighty ghosts stride through the halls of the Lodge. James Stewart and Marilyn Monroe. Clark Gable and Norma Shearer. Gary Cooper and Claudette Colbert. Joan Bennett and David O. Selznick. These are only a few of the personalities you'll see staring at you from photographs of the yesterdays they were skiing Sun Valley.

Ernest Hemingway finished one of his greatest novels, *For Whom the Bell Tolls*, in room 206 at the Lodge. He bought a home in Sun Valley and his children were born and raised there. A small memorial was erected to him after he took his own life nearby. You pass it in a grove of trees on a cross-country trail.

Though memories haunt Sun Valley, it's not an aging beauty of yesterday but an outstanding resort that still captivates the celebrities. Brooke Shields and Clint Eastwood and Janet Leigh and Arnold Schwarzenegger are among the many luminaries who maintain hideaway homes there today.

Sun Valley gave the skiers of the world a magnificent gift of the day it opened: the chairlift. It was invented here.

Today there are 13 lifts, including 7 high-speed quads. The Challenger quad whisks skiers up a 3,1000-foot vertical in only 10 minutes. A computerized state-of-the-art snowmaking system assures skiers of fun on 80 percent of the slopes by mid-November.

Sun Valley is actually four areas.

One is the original showplace Lodge—now the centerpiece of Sun Valley Village, with stores, art shops, restaurants, and the gracious Sun Valley Inn.

Another, almost across the street, is the old mining and cowboy town of Ketchum, where you'll find the hottest nightspots and gourmet restaurants, including Hemingway's favorite, the Pioneer Saloon. Ranchers still buy horseshoes and machinery parts next door to boutiques where visitors shop for glistening skis and elegant après-ski boots.

Condominiums and private homes are scattered between Ketchum and Warm Springs, at the base of Old Baldy.

A third area is Elkhorn, near Dollar Mountain, a village in its own right with a variety of lodgings and a cluster of shops.

And the fourth is incomparable Old Baldy, a roundish mountain of long intermediate and black runs, and the adjacent Seattle Ridge. For those with the stamina, it's possible to ski from the 9,140-foot summit in a single long swoop to the base without losing the thrill by skiing flat interconnecting runs. Dollar Mountain, in a range of mountains across the valley from Old Baldy, is where the experts skied a half century ago. Now it's an exemplary beginner's learning slope.

Old Baldy offers skiers the unique option of skiing all day in the sun, starting on the east-facing runs on the Warm Springs side in the morning and ending the day on the west-facing River Run trails.

Sun Valley welcomes snowboarders, who have their own half-pipe and snowboard park for thrills. Twenty-five km of marked and groomed cross-country trails range from golf-course flats to expert mountain trails.

Among the many off-slope activities is the opportunity to take a cross-country ski trek to a Mongolian yurt for a sumptuous dinner, then an unforgettable trip back at night. Or to ride in a horse-drawn sleigh through the star-studded darkness to eat a classic western feast at an ancient, restored ranch house.

With Sun Valley's location at the edge of the mighty Sawtooth Mountains, you can get off a lift at the summit and stare in awe at an endless ocean of mountain peaks.

One of the resort's advantages over some of the other outstanding destination playgrounds in the West is its base elevation, 5,740 feet; skiers don't have to spend a couple days acclimatizing themselves to the altitude.

For information and reservations, call (800) 622-4111; for snow conditions, (800) 635-4150. Or write Sun Valley Company, Sun Valley, ID 83353. On the Internet: www.sunvalley.com.

Vail

Vail is a resort put together with superlatives. Whatever can be said of it today will be revised, enlarged, or improved tomorrow.

For skiing, it's among the most imposing areas in North America. There are two main sides to the long Vail Mountain masiff—the "front face," which faces the village, and the "back bowls."

The dozens of consistently groomed runs on the front face, with a 3,300-foot vertical, are a playground for intermediates with enough interesting drops to keep an expert satisfied. One-third of the mountain's endless trails weaving through the trees are a joy for beginners and novices.

The back bowls consist of a fabulous 6-mile-wide stretch of treeless terrain. More than two-thirds of the bowls are classified as for advanced skiers. The rest are for courageous intermediates.

The 25 lifts can carry 40,000 skiers an hour. They include nine high-speed detachable quads, one six-passenger gondola, one fixed-grip quad, three triple chairlifts, six double chairlifts, and five surface lifts.

For shredders who want to carve the corduroy, Vail's half-pipe for snowboarders is one of the world's largest, and the jibline's metal and wood rail slides are popular with the experts. So, too, is "earth surfing" the deep-powder back bowls.

As a destination resort Vail is one of the world's most upscale ski areas.

The village is charming. Its narrow streets are lined with ski boutiques—where sales may feature discounts on chic, $5,000 fur ski jackets—art galleries, which display the works of outstanding artists in every medium, and specialty stores selling handmade Native American artifacts along with handmade cowboy boots and authentic western wear. Housing includes elegant hotels, condos, and chalets. There are more than 50 restaurants, from the lavish and truly gourmet to pizza parlors and sidewalk cafés.

Vail.

Modestly priced facilities within a reasonable driving distance are at a minimum.

Après-ski life runs from full gamut from swinging discos to saloons with an Old West flavor, and from discreet piano bars to a refuge featuring Austrian folk music.

Vail has the nation's largest snowboarding school, along with extensive ski school facilities.

There are two nurseries and day-care centers for the wee ones from 2 months to 6 years, and ski schools for kids from 3 to 12. Teens have their own programs. A fabled "Kids Only" ski trail winds around Indian wigwams, log forts, trading posts, and saloons, and through a mine.

Off the slopes, almost every conceivable winter activity is available, including a cross-country ski trip on the 10th Mountain Division trail, which runs from Vail to Aspen. The trail was named for the famed 10th Mountain Division, which trained for Alpine warfare during World War II at Camp Hale, 30 miles from Vail.

Intelligently, Vail, with a base elevation of 7,000 feet, offers skiers in its vacation planning guide advice on how to minimize altitude problems.

Direct flights into Vail/Eagle airport, 30 miles from the slopes, are available from seven major American cities. Vail is 100 miles west of Denver on Interstate 70.

For information, write for the Vail Planning Guide, Vail, CO 81658; or call (970) 476-9090. On the Internet: http://vail.net. On e-mail: vail-bcr@vail.net.

Whistler/Blackcomb

Put two great ski mountains side by side, each with more than 5,000 feet of vertical—the most in North America—and you've got the first hint of what it's like to play on the slopes of Whistler/Blackcomb, 75 miles north of Vancouver, British Columbia.

Cover them with 200 marked trails on 6,998 acres of skiable terrain and you'll begin to sense why this dual resort area is one that an increasing number of Americans are as determined as their Canadian ski friends to keep secret. Their efforts are an abysmal failure.

Then give skiers everything from endless miles of easy greens to low intermediate to top expert trails, glacier skiing, wide bowls, steep glades, and some nonstop runs that weave and wind from their summits, each

Whistler/Blackcomb.

about 1,500 feet above treeline, to their bases, and you'll understand why both *Snow Country* and *Ski* magazine readers consider this the outstanding ski resort complex in North America.

Here's an enticing summary of the skiing:

Whistler has an elevation of 7,165 feet and a vertical drop of 5,020 feet. Neighbor Blackcomb has an elevation of 7,494 feet and a vertical of 5,280 feet. The base elevation is 2,145 feet. On both, the skiing above timberline is, basically, for high intermediates and experts only. There are seven alpine bowls, one of which is a glacier, on Whistler; five bowls, two of which are glaciers, on Blackcomb. These offer better skiers unlimited ways to get down from the summit.

Since the resort is almost adjacent to the ocean, there are more cloudy days on the two mountains than is usual at ski resorts.

Blackcomb is served by one eight-person gondola, six quads, three triple chairlifts, and three surface lifts. Whistler has a 10-person gondola, four high-speed quads, three triple chairlifts, one double, and five surface lifts. More are planned.

While the two mountains are separated by the steep Fitzsimmons Valley, the lifts link up at the base of each gondola. For the summer enthusiasts, two ski lifts and half-pipes for shredders are open on Blackcomb's Horstman Glacier from mid-June to August.

Whistler/Blackcomb has a rich variety of excellent teaching programs for skiers as well as snowboarders.

There are 28 km of cross-country groomed track runs that range from nothing more difficult than a golf course to the expert level.

Child care is available for infants as young as 18 months. There are lessons, private and group, for the 5-to-12-year-olds. At night, the young-sters have their own ball in the Wonderland Amusement Arcade with everything from video games to pool tables.

The "town" of Whistler—really three villages with some 150 shops—is remarkably similar to the quaint ski resorts of Europe, with chalets, condominiums, ski houses, and small B&Bs. Perhaps half have ski-in, ski-out convenience. All are connected by local buses.

It's impossible to go hungry at Whistler/Blackcomb. Between them the two areas have 15 on-mountain cafeterias, pizza parlors, and restaurants, ranging from the expensive and elegant to a hamburger joint, with an international variety of cuisine.

The après-ski scene is a bit less roaring than you'd anticipate in the Canadian mountains, with modest bars stirring things up in the early evening; a few noisy pubs grind out the decibels beginning around 10 o'clock.

Finally, there's one other wonderful factor for Americans: You pay in Canadian dollars. For several years these have ranged from 20 to 30 percent cheaper than American dollars. Non-Canadian visitors also get back the 7 percent goods and service tax that's applied to everything you buy, from lift tickets to housing, though not to what you eat or drink.

Vancouver airport is served nonstop from most major U.S. and international cities. Whistler/Blackcomb can be reached by train or interurban buses from Vancouver, or by private car.

For resort information and reservations, call (800) 944-7853; fax: (604) 932-7231.

Appendices

Who invented downhill skiing as we know it today? A Skiing enthusiast, Lawday, has the delightful answer. It may surprise you.

A HISTORY OF ALPINE SKIING, SORT OF*
BY DAVID LAWDAY

Looking down, from an aircraft, at mountains in winter. The world below is grand, mysterious, white and empty. You could ski forever, it seems, without meeting a soul. This is not wholly illusion. If space were the only requirement, there need be almost no limit to the growth of skiing, even in Europe's busy Alps. It is a sport for hero and coward, speed-merchant and bumbler. The thrills and chills are not all in the pace of the skis underfoot. They are in the raw beauty of the mountain setting.

The notion that sliding down snow is more entertaining than sliding across it on the flat only dawned on people at the end of the last century. It seems, in retrospect, an absurdly simple proposition to have escaped mountain folk down the ages. Once recognized, however, it caused doctrinal schisms of the kind that have rent religions. The embattled sport of downhill skiing did not properly establish itself until after the second world war, when people became rich again and were seeking new fun.

Downhill skiing, now known as Alpine skiing, has spread fast in a short life. Some 45 million people around the world do it, wherever snow covers mountains. The Japanese are among the most numerous skiers,

*Reprinted from *The Economist*, of London.

followed by the Americans, French and West Germans. The Swiss and Austrians are, as nations, the keenest. Indians do it in Kashmir, Chileans in the Andes, Lebanese on their peaks above the Mediterranean. The cradle of the sport is the jagged Alpine range that arches spectacularly across Austria and Switzerland into eastern France and northern Italy. The main centers of Alpine skiing are there and in the America Rockies, so this survey concentrates on those two areas.

Alpine skiing grew around the British, who have no mountains to speak of but like organizing other people. At first, their true winter sports were mountaineering, skating and tobogganing. These pursuits took the Victorian upper class to Alpine towns, which welcomed their custom and named hotels after them. By the 1880s the British were contriving amusements like the Cresta (toboggan) Run at St. Moritz, which, in the age before motor cars or aeroplanes, was the fastest thing on earth. Rattling down the ice at 130 kilometers per hour would then have felt, and still feels, like twice that speed with eyes and nose riding only blurred centimeters above the track. . . .

None of this was meant for Alpine locals (though Swiss and Germans, when permitted to ride, can be good at it). Alpine folk used skins, slatted squares of wood, or racket-style snowshoes to get around their steepest slopes. Skiing was something done by Norwegians and other Nordic folk to traverse their flat winter wastes and, when the spirit moved them, to jump. The Norwegians had been skiing like that since Adam. Skis were an essential arm of warfare in Nordic countries back in the early Middle Ages. Nansen, an Arctic explorer, used skis on his freezing polar adventures in the late nineteenth century. His exploits fascinated Europe. His cross-country method, using heavy wooden planks up to nine feet in length, created a following even in the Alps. Ski associations sprang up to see what recreation it could offer.

Nobody turned corners on these skis. It could not be done. It was bad form to try. Enthusiasts, known as 'ski-runners,' sat astride a stout pole like a witch on a broomstick and pressed down upon it to brake themselves. Because of the steepness of the Alps, they sometimes had to tackle fast descents. The journal of the Austrian Ski Association for 1892–93 describes it thus:

"On the descent the ski runner leans back on this stick and shuts his eyes. He darts downwards as straight as an arrow until he can no longer breathe. He then throws himself sideways on the snow, and waits until he regains his breath before once again hurling himself downwards. . . ."

Turning would clearly have spoiled the fun. But there were no pistes then, and no skiing hordes to get in the way.

Zdarsky and Crouch

A reclusive Austrian, Mathias Zdarsky, determined that turning would help. He spent several winters in a solitary beginner's class as teacher and student, devising a ski-binding that fixed the foot without restricting the heel. He discovered that if he pushed down on the heel and included his body in a certain way, the ski automatically turned. This meant that he could ski without falling however steep the terrain, even between the pine trees. The only drawback was that he could not go very fast.

In a technical book published in 1897, this pioneer of the turn—and hence of Alpine skiing itself—told the Austrian Ski Association what was wrong with the technique learned from the Norwegians. The experts turned resentful. A colonel in the imperial Austrian army, who regarded the proposed alternative as an insult, challenged him to a duel. It was the first engagement in the holy wars over style that have marked skiing's evolution ever since. Rival claims to paternity of the sport added to the conflict. A score of towns around the Alps which had not heard much of Zdarsky claimed to have invented Alpine skiing. The climate was rather like that accompanying the invention of photography, or the telephone: nobody had wanted Nicephore Niepce or Alexander Graham Bell to hog all the credit.

None of this went unnoticed by well-born British travelers in the Alps. Although downhill skiing was still roundly despised by its many critics, they organized in 1911 the first downhill ski championship, at Crans-Montana, Switzerland. There were no lifts. To get to the start, competitors had to tramp uphill for hours. The race, called the Kandahar (as it still is), was named after Lord Roberts of Kandahar, a pillar of the British Raj in India known for his campaigns against Afghanistan. His noble name was borrowed, it seems, because it conjured up Afghanistan's mountainous landscape and because it would surely help attract enough of the right kind of competitors.

The competition did not halt objections to downhill skiing, which for some time continued to be widely regarded as a pastime for those too *cowardly to jump in the prodigious Norwegian style or too feeble to enter cross-country races. Arnold Lunn, son of a Victorian travel agent, Henry Lunn, put Alpine skiing on a surer footing by organizing the first international slalom race at Murren, Switzerland, in 1922.*

The word slalom *was taken from Norwegian, which in itself must have irritated cross-country diehards. Arnold Lunn's race was meant to be all rhythmic turns, requiring a deliberate style that the rough-and-tumble Kandahar, a sort of fell-running contest on snow, did not encourage. He drew up a downhill racing rule-book to go with it. Using sticks for braking was forbidden, a rule which the Austrian and Swiss ski associations opposed as artificial. They thought it was overbearing of the British, who skied badly, to depart from precedents set by Nordic people who skied well.*

The Austrian, born to the mountains, could also see that winter sports were a class-conscious affair for the British. Arnold (later Sir Arnold) Lunn was rejected for membership in the Ski Club of Great Britain when he first applied; he was 'trade.' He was the first person blackballed by the club, which was founded in 1903. He managed to get in later and presided over the club (which retains avuncular influence in the skiing world). Getting Alpine skiing fully legitimized was more difficult. It was not brought into the Winter Olympic Games to stand with traditional Nordic events until 1936.

ADDENDA

Whatever you want to know about ski resorts, alpine skiing, cross-country trails, or snowboarding you can find somewhere—in specialized magazines, books, videocassettes, or, now, the Internet.

Cyberspace

The new open-sesame for skiers is the World Wide Web. On it you will find everything from detailed profiles of individual resorts to services that report comprehensively on ski areas throughout the world, from Alaska to New Zealand, Japan to Europe, and every country in between.

Check out Skinet (www.skinet.com), a service of *Ski* and *Skiing* magazines. Reports range from profiles of ski resorts throughout the country to World Cup results and today's snow conditions.

Snow Country's Home Page (www.snocountry.com) provides current ski conditions and general information on special events at ski areas without charge. From this site, users can be hyperlinked to dozens of ski areas with their own individual reports.

Weather Service International operates INTELLiCast, (www.intelli-cast.com), which offers free real-time and forecasted weather reports from ski areas, plus ski conditions, trail maps, and profiles of ski areas in every area of the world.

Resort Sports Network (www.rsn.com) gives the eager skier a peek through live video cameras at what's going on right now at the areas it serves.

Ski America's service (www.skiamerica.com) has profiles on ski areas throughout the United States and Canada, with current ski conditions.

Many individual resorts will give you a complex online questionnaire for everything you may want to know—from bars to bedrooms, special events to ski packages—about booking a holiday at their area. Fill it out and within 24 hours you'll receive suggestions on e-mail.

One question that occasionally arises among skiers who ski the Web is the accuracy of reports on snow conditions at a resort they're planning to visit shortly. Some have a reputation for a bit of fudging. But Phil Camp, director of Snow Country Reports, which puts together the daily information on conditions around the world, says, "The data the ski resorts feed in every day are, on the whole, quite accurate.

"If we have any reason to doubt a report, it's not put online until it can be verified.

"You can believe them."

Books

Excellent information on all the major and many of the gem resorts can be found in annually updated ski guidebooks. These include:

Peak Ski Guide & Travel Planner—United States and Canada, "The Official Ski Area Guide of U.S. Skiing." Probably the most comprehensive guide published, this lists vital statistics on 704 alpine ski areas, including peak elevation, vertical, number of trails, number of and types of lifts, percentage of snowmaking, longest trail, night skiing hours, average season, adult lift-ticket prices for downhill and maintained cross-country trails, facilities for snowboarders, and costs of rentals, lessons, and day care, along with such amenities as housing, restaurants, bars, and cafeterias, and how to get there by plane, train, or car.

Two hundred thirteen of the larger areas are described in text and/or trail maps. Indicative of the descriptions is how it begins its comments on Colorado's Purgatory: "In Purgatory you're just a chairlift away from Heaven-on-Earth. . . . [This] is an immensely enjoyable mountain, lots of 'white gold,' spectacular San Juan scenery, and days upon days of Southwestern sunshine—Eureka indeed!"

Embassy Imprint, 142 Ferry Road, Old Saybrook, CT 06475; (203) 395-0188.

Skiing America, by Charles Leocha, profiles 75 major North American resorts, describing what they offer in skiing and amenities. Included is an overall introduction to each area, and details on: where to ski; the mountain rating, a description of the general terrain; cross-country skiing and rates; ski school prices; lift-ticket prices; accommodations, with descriptions and prices of condominiums, lodges, chalets, and inns; dining, with names and prices of outstanding restaurants; child-care facilities; and reservations.

It begins its comments on Mount Snow, Vermont: "Mount Snow has the snowmaking efficiency of Killington and is closer to major cities than Stratton, and has just as careful grooming, but somehow this resort has remained about as down-home and folksy and unpretentious as all Vermont resorts should be."

Ski Europe, also by Charles Leocha, offers similar reports on what it describes as the "best ski vacations at over 75 European resorts."

Both books are available from World Leisure Corporation, 177 Paris Street, Boston, MA 02128; (617) 569-1966; fax (617) 561-7654.

The White Book of Ski Areas, by Robert Enzel, is a bare-bones report on every ski area in North and South America with essential information on what each offers. The data is easier to read here than in the *Peak Guide.* However, the *White Book* doesn't include any descriptive profiles of resorts.

Inter-Ski Services, P.O. Box 9595, Friendship Station, Washington, DC 20016; (202) 342-0886; fax (202) 338-1940.

Skiing USA: The Insider's Guide, by Clive Hobson. One of the Fodor travel books, this covers the top 30 resorts in the United States. The emphasis is on the overall resort, but with good detail on the skiing. As with travel books generally, it has a lot of nice things to say about each area.

Regional Guides

There also are regional ski guidebooks for those who already know the particular area where they intend to try the slopes. Among them are:

Rocky Mountain Skiing, by Claire Walter, Western Editor of *Skiing* magazine. This is an outstanding book on the region, written with a sprightly flair by a ski travel expert who really knows the territory. It treats fairly and equally the amenities and skiing at each of the areas covered without overloading the reader with meaningless superlatives.

Fulcrum Publishing, (800) 992-2908.

The Access Guide series has expanded its coverage from cities to ski areas. It's now publishing two: *Western United States* and *Eastern United States.* There are short and informative write-ups on individual areas, with sharp and revealing comments about the "bests" in each.

Harper Perennial Publishing, (800) 331-3761.

Skier's Guide to Utah, by Michael Jensen, should prove increasingly popular now that the state is set to host the Winter Olympics in 2002. There are trail maps of each area, and a lot of good details about every resort in the Beehive State.

Gulf Publishing Company, (713) 520-4444.

Magazines

Facts and fantasies, way-out stories and intimate descriptions of ski resorts, annual guides to the newest ski equipment and clothing, dramatic color photographs of skiers doing the impossible, and advice on every facet of alpine and cross-country skiing and snowboarding are contained in the indispensable ski magazines, including:

Ski and *Skiing,* published by Times Mirror Magazines, 2 Park Avenue, New York, NY 10016.

Snowboard Life, especially for snowboarders over the age of 25, and *Transworld Snowboarding,* for snowboarders 15 to 16, published by Times Mirror Magazines, 353 Airport Road, Oceanside, CA 92054; (619) 722-7777.

Snow Country, published by Sports/Leisure Magazines, 5520 Park Avenue, P.O. Box 395, Trumbull, CT 06611-0395; (203) 373-7000.

Powder, "The Skier's Magazine," published by Surfer Publications, Box 1028, Dana Point, CA 92629; (714) 496-5922; fax (714) 496-7849.

Snowboarder, published by Surfer Publications, 33046 Calle Aviador, San Juan Capistrano, CA 92675.

Ski Tech, issued five times yearly, and *Ski Racing, Ski Racing Annual, Ski Show Daily,* and *New England Skiers Guide,* published by Ski Racing International, Box 1125, Route 100, Waitsfield, VT 05673; (802) 496-7700; fax (802) 496-7704.

Videocassettes

Training videos, for everyone from beginner to expert, are widely available. Among those concerned basically with alpine skiing are *Parallel Skiing Made Easy,* produced by Tyrolia and voiced by Martin Hechlaman, and *Learn to Ski Better,* by Warren Miller, producer of some of the world's most exciting extreme ski films. The Miller production ranges from instruction for beginners to the intricacies of mastering moguls.

Among tapes for the more advanced skiers are *Breakthrough on Skis, or How to Get Out of the Intermediate Rut* and *Breakthrough II, Bumps & Powder Simplified,* produced by Lito Tejada-Flores, a contributing editor to *Skiing* magazine.

Index